'NO TRIFLING MATTER'

Being an Account of a Voyage by Emigrants from Sussex and Hampshire — to — Upper Canada on board the 'BRITISH TAR' in 1834.

Edited by Sheila Haines.

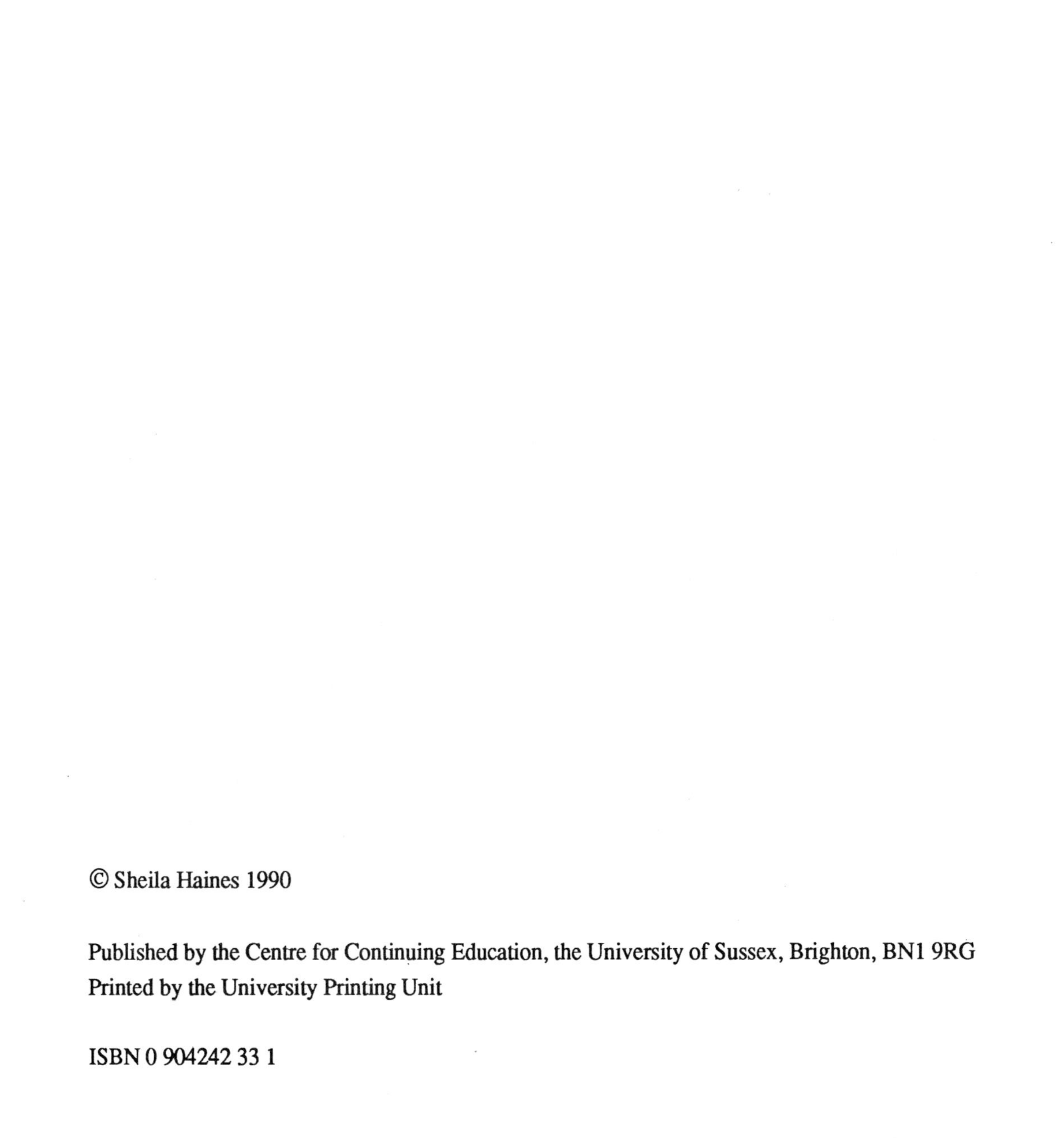

Published by the Centre for Continuing Education, the University of Sussex, Brighton, BN1 9RG
Printed by the University Printing Unit

ISBN 0 904242 33 1

CONTENTS

ILLUSTRATIONS

Illustration Sources. *Title page:* designed by Richard Lawson; *Pages 1 and 11:* from 1800 Woodcuts by Thomas Bewick and his School (Dover Publications Inc.); *pages 2, 5, 24, 27, 39, 43:* Petworth House Archives; *pages 4, 17, 28:* West Sussex Record Office; *page 7:* Hampshire County Library, Portsmouth Reproductions of Old Prints; *page 8:* Cynthia Jeffrey; *pages 10, 13, 19, 34:* Illustrated London News 1849; *page 18:* Trustees of the Goodwood Collection; *page 21:* Illustrated London News 1850; *page 25:* Illustrated London News 1844; *pages 30 and 33:* Illustrations by George Cruikshank to Dibdin's Sea Songs, (2nd Ed. (1841); *page 35:* R.H. Bonnycastle, The Canadas in 1841 (Henry Colburn); *pages 41 and 42:* C.P. Homung, Handbook of Early Advertising Art (Mainly from American Sources) (Dover Publications Inc.); *page 48:* A cartoon by Leech in Punch 1848.

No Trifling Matter owes its existence to a University of Sussex Centre for Continuing Education and Workers Educational Association six week history workshop that took place in Worthing in the summer of 1988. A seemingly lighthearted addition to a longer winter course on emigration from Great Britain in the 19th century, this short course soon proved to be indeed no trifling matter, spreading into months rather than weeks and involving a good deal of time, attention and energy on the part of the group members.

We have tried to portray the experiences of some of the men, women and children who emigrated from Sussex and Hampshire to Canada in 1834 on one particular ship, the *British Tar*. Such emigrants figure in official reports and archives, at best as mere names, at worst as a number. To give such people flesh and blood, histories and feelings of their own is difficult for the records they left are sparse, and we are aware of the many gaps that remain in our account. Nevertheless, many of the emigrants who sailed away from Portsmouth on the *British Tar*, on 17 April 1834 are now, for us, people whom we begin to know and appreciate.

We have taken our travellers to Ontario and, apart from two later letters home, have left them at that point. We hope to learn what happened to some of them in later years. Research is underway both here, and in Toronto, which could eventually cast some light on the fate of the prolific West family; the boy, George Sheppard; the newborn Ditton baby; Elizabeth and Cornelius Voice and their fellow emigrants flooding into Canada in the 1830s.

Our acknowledgements and thanks are due to Barbara Brydone, Cynthia Jeffrey, Richard Lawson, Dr D.L. Phillips M.R.C.S., L.R.C.P., Fred Gray., R.Wood M.P.S., Anna Clarke, The East Sussex Record Office, the Isle of Wight County Record Office, the S.P.C.K., the West Sussex Record Office, the Worthing Branch of the W.E.A., and our long suffering kith and kin. We give especial thanks to Lord Egremont for permission to quote from and reproduce material from the Petworth House Archives. All quotations and reproductions from the Goodwood Collections are by courtesy of the Trustees of the Goodwood Collections and with acknowledgements to the West Sussex Record Office and the County Archivist.

Sheila Haines

The members of the group who researched and wrote this book were Brian Cave, Margaret Gardiner, Don Green, Sheila Haines, Charles Howick, Joan Howick, Leigh Lawson, Maureen Prangnell and Vera Townsend.

OUTWARD BOUND

The Earl of Egremont

has signified his intention of continuing his liberal assistance to persons wishing to emigrate to

UPPER CANADA.

The COMMITTEE will therefore engage a vessel to sail from PORTSMOUTH, *early in April next*, under similar arrangements as those of 1832 and 1833.

Applications for Passages should be made as early as possible to

J. PHILLIPS,

LIBRARY, PETWORTH.

Petworth, Feb. 14th. 1834.

Phillips, Printer, Petworth.

1:LEAVING HOME

In the early months of 1834 a Billingshurst family were preparing to embark on the most momentous journey of their lives. They were to leave Sussex and sail from Portsmouth on 17 April aboard the small sailing brig the *British Tar* for the long voyage to Canada.

The family's name was Voice, Cornelius, a carpenter and joiner; Elizabeth his wife; their four sons William, aged 23, Cornelius, aged 14, George and Joseph both under 11, a fifth son and a nephew one of whom was called John; Elizabeth, aged 16, and Martha, aged 12, their two younger daughters. Their eldest child, Mary, did not go with them. Elizabeth and Cornelius were stout hearted to contemplate such a journey. Very possibly they had hitherto never been far from their area of Sussex. Emigration to Canada was a giant step into the unknown, the preparations for their journey must have been tremendous.

The *British Tar* had been chartered by the Petworth Emigration Committee, a body which had been the inspiration of the Reverend Thomas Sockett, the Rector of Petworth, and financed by the Third Earl of Egremont of Petworth House. This Committee was set up to assist the emigration to Canada of unemployed farm labourers, skilled agricultural workers, artisans and others wishing to emigrate. The ship was small and Cornelius, Elizabeth and their children would be spending seven weeks in the extremely cramped steerage quarters in the hold. A six foot square berth would be allocated to every three adults, or six children under the age of 14, above the lower berths would be a second tier, so that the headroom between the two was only two to three feet. In such conditions the emigrants would have to live much of their time until they reached Montreal, when they would have a further journey of three weeks by boat and wagon before they arrived at their new home in Blandford, Upper Canada - now the state of Ontario.

Such a journey in such conditions was 'no trifling matter' as Sockett was himself to admit [(1)] and careful preparation and packing was important. Elizabeth and Cornelius could get practical advice from pamphlets on sale in Petworth, which drew upon the experiences of earlier emigrants, and also from the instructions issued by the P.E.C.itself. The lists given by the latter for necessary clothing and household goods were extremely comprehensive; many emigrants had probably never owned so many clothes before.

List of Necessaries for Emigrants to Upper Canada:

Families should take: bedding, blankets, sheets etc., pewter plates or wooden trenchers, knives, forks, spoons, metal cups and mugs, tea kettles and saucepans, a large tin can or watering pot, and working tools of all descriptions.

Single men must have: a bed or mattress, a metal plate, cup or mug, a knife, fork and spoon.

A bed tick rather than a feather bed was recommended for the journey. The tick could be stuffed with straw, and an old piece of carpet put under the tick would help to keep the occupant warm.

Clothing: the following was the 'lowest outfit recommended to Parishes for their labourers including any such other articles they possess'.

A Fur cap
A warm great coat
A flushing jacket and trousers
A canvas frock and 2 pairs of trousers
A duck frock and trousers
Two jersey frocks
Four shirts
Four pairs of stockings
Three pairs of shoes
A Bible and Prayer book
Women were to have the same in proportion and especially a ***warm*** *cloak* [(2)]

A flushing jacket was made out of rough, thick woollen cloth, as worn in Flushing, a port in Holland.

Under the Petworth scheme prospective emigrants were to be funded in these purchases by their parish. Petworth emigrants, for example, sponsored by the Earl of Egremont were granted £5 a head, £3.10s. for a child, from the Petworth poor relief funds. The P.E.C. urged other parishes and sponsors to do the same for it would not do 'to let the people go with Lord Egremont's name attached to them, in a beggarly condition'[(3)]. Nevertheless, some parishes did grind the sum down to £4 or £3.10s.or less. The poor law authorities on the Isle of Wight seem to have incurred extra expenses when they had to redeem would - be emigrants' own clothing from pawn. Maybe they docked this money from the clothing grant. The West Sussex emigrants were urged to buy their goods from tradesmen in Petworth itself - a useful boost to local trade. Mr Chrippes, a member of the P.E.C., could supply many of the goods, presumably from a store at his auctioneer's office. Any money left over from the £5 grant, and any personal money, was put into an account and kept by the Superintendent in charge of the *British Tar* party to be repaid when the emigrants reached Montreal.

Captain J.C. Hale, who had supervised emigrant ships to Canada in 1832 and 1833, had written detailed *Instructions to Persons intending to emigrate...* a two-penny pamphlet published by the Petworth printer, J.Phillips.[4] Cornelius would be wise, for example, to take nails and screws to fix into the wooden bulkhead above his berth for use as hangers for clothing, and boxes in which to store little things such as cutlery, which might otherwise roll around the pitching steerage and be lost. As a carpenter Cornelius would doubtless be skilful at making the most of all available space, and like all craftsmen would have great affinity with his own tools; his 'most important possessions'. Hale especially recommended that carpenters should take saws of all kinds with them, they were of doubtful quality and expensive to buy in Canada.

Elizabeth should choose and pack her household goods carefully. She should take only little articles of practical use, scissors, sewing and knitting needles, thread and worsted yarn. These, and small items such as salt cellars, should be stowed in saucepans and other domestic utensils. Large and bulky goods would prove a constant incumbrance and expensive to transport up the country. Two very worthwhile items, Hale suggested, were a Dutch oven and small trivet to hang on the bars of the cooking hearth on board ship. The P.E.C. provided basic rations on the voyage but the passengers would have to cook these themselves. A quart tin pot with a flat side and a hook to hang it on the stove would be useful for boiling a little water.

In addition to the food provided by the P.E.C. Elizabeth would doubtless try to take some of the supplementary provisions suggested by Hale. These could include eggs, packed little end downwards in salt to preserve them; portable soup; jam; dried fruit; gingerbread; pickles; dried yeast; and perhaps a small chest of tea - expensive but comforting. Some of these goods would come from Elizabeth's own store and maybe relatives would present her with others. She may well have taken some of her own household nostrums. Hale recommended peppermint drops and carraway seeds for 'when the children are a little qualmish' and suggested a supply of a new kind of soap for use with salt water. With such cramped conditions on board ship cleanliness was to be important.

There had been much contemporary scepticism over letters coming back to England from supposed emigrants. People doubted they were genuine. This was understandable, for many emigrants and their families at home would be illiterate and dependent on others writing letters for them. How was the recipient to be sure that a letter in a strange hand was from whom it purported to be? Emigration agencies and interested authorities were also suspected of issuing their own versions of emigrants' letters painting Canada as a highly desirable destination. Intending emigrants devised methods to combat such doubts. Elizabeth and Cornelius could take precautions before they left by tearing a strip off their writing paper and leaving it at home with the intended recipient to be matched when a letter arrived, or by asking the intended recipient to write their own name at the head of the writing paper that the emigrant would eventually send.

Having completed the practical preparations for the journey there remained one very important package:

Emigrants should take with them a good character (if they have the happiness to possess one) fairly written and well-attested, also copies of marriage and baptismal registers or any other certificates or papers likely to be useful: the whole to be enclosed in a small tin case.[5]

So now, all goodbyes to the family and friends having been said, all luggage made ready, the family was set for the journey to Portsmouth and embarkation on the *British Tar*. They travelled, most probably, by road but possibly partly by sea from Shoreham, and had to be in Portsmouth by noon on 16 April, the day before their ship was due to sail.

Pulboro' 14th April 1834.

I the undersigned hereby acknowledge this day receiving the sum of five pounds of the Parish officers of Pulboro', money advanced me to clothe myself & family on going to Canada. —

£5..0-0

Witness. W Blunden

Wm Green

THE

British Tar,

A 1. coppered and copper fastened,

383 TONS registered Burthen,

is engaged by

The Petworth Emigration Committee,

to sail from

Portsmouth,

FOR

Montreal, direct,

On THURSDAY, APRIL 17th.

A few first and second Cabin Berths may be had, by *early* application, and further Particulars known of the PRINTER,

. Phillips, Petworth.

March 18th. 1834.

2:PORTSMOUTH

Waiting for them at Portsmouth was the Reverend Thomas Sockett who moved down to the port on Monday 14 April, three days before the ship was due to depart, and stayed at 20 Penney Street, a stone's throw from the harbour.

Sockett was to later claim that he had been the active hand behind the whole Petworth plan; 'with the assistance of two parishioners of mine' although it had been 'Lord Egremont's purse' that provided the money.[6] This may well have been true for when the scheme was launched in 1832 Egremont was already 81 years old and was to die in 1837 after the seventh, and final P.E.C. ship, had sailed from Portsmouth. The *British Tar* was the fourth ship that Sockett had organised and despatched. The *Lord Melville* and the *Eveline* sailed in 1832 and the *England* in 1833. Sockett had by then been Rector of Petworth for 18 years. He also held the livings of nearby Duncton and a parish in Lincolnshire. He began his ministry at Northchapel and owed his ordination and livings to the patronage of Egremont for whom he had worked, from the age of 19,as tutor to Egremont's three young sons. Sockett was an influential person in Petworth and conscientious in his concern for his parishioners; '...who were boys with myself; men whose habits I know into whose cottages I frequently walk, and at the side of whose fire I often sit.'[7] He was Chairman of Petworth Vestry, and administered poor law relief in the town, prior to 1835, for 20 years.

His promotion of emigration as a cure for the contemporary spectre of a growing 'surplus population'; agricultural unemployment and distress; increasing taxation and claims for poor relief; and the coming rigours of new poor law regulations in 1834, was a mixture of humanitarian feeling and economic and social expediency. He could write to the Duke of Richmond in coldly pragmatic terms of the need for 'relieving parishes of their plethora'[8] and describe labourers' children in harsh threatening terms as:

...a burthen to their parents, and a nuisance to their neighbours: numbers,from absolute want of employment, becoming first pilferers, then poachers, and eventually thieves upon a larger scale; crowding our prisons with juvenile offenders, and adding, at a fearfully increasing rate, to the accumulating mass of crime and misery .[9]

Such attitudes were, nevertheless, coupled with a genuine wish that people like Elizabeth and Cornelius Voice should have a better life and wider opportunities for their children:

By enduring a few weeks of inconvenience and fatigue, they are elevated to a class in society, far above that they before occupied...By emigrating to Canada he gets at once into a situation,where...a large family is really a treasure to a man: and where by industry and care ...he will be able to lay up for himself, repose and comfort in the decline of life:- may see his children and his children's children flocking around him...[10]

So Sockett wrote in a *Letter* to Members of Parliament and other authorities urging them to sponsor schemes of emigration in a relatively humane and civilised fashion. Nevertheless, he devoted a considerable part of this pamphlet to pointing out the desirable economics of encouraging poor families to emigrate rather then keeping them out of parish poor rates. He may, of course, have been realistic in this approach suspecting that appeals to economy would be the most telling way of interesting influential men and parish officials in emigration schemes. Sockett could not be accused of too high handedly advocating emigration only for others for he had a son, George, who had gone to Canada in 1833.

The 'purse' behind the P.E.C. the Third Earl of Egremont had a great reputation as a philanthropist at a national and local level. He paid the fare of £10 outright for people wishing to emigrate with the P.E.C. from Petworth itself and the neighbouring parishes of Duncton, Northchapel, Egdean and Tillington, and was willing to pay part of the £10 in proportion to the land he owned in other parishes. Paying, for example, one fifth of the expense for Lurgashall and one thirty-sixth for Pulborough.

By 1834 it seemed that the number of people wishing to go, or being persuaded to do so, from Petworth and its immediate neighbourhood had, for the time being, been drained away on earlier ships, and many of the passengers on the *British Tar* came from further afield. As well as 43 passengers from the Isle of Wight, there were emigrants from more distant parts of West and East Sussex. Those from the Isle of Wight were largely sent by the poor law guardians. Some East Sussex parishes paid the expenses of their emigrants partly from the poor law rate and partly by loans from local landowners such as the Earl of Chichester at Stanmer, and Thomas Calverley of Hellingly. Some local landowners and business men seem to have paid outright. We do not know who paid for the Voice family. Living in Billingshurst they fell outside Egremont's bounty. There is no record of them ever having parish relief.

Indeed, Cornelius was himself a member of Billingshurst Vestry, and as a rate payer and craftsman he may have been able to raise the fare for himself and his family, although this would have been in the region of £80, a considerable amount of money. Possibly his older sons paid for themselves, and other members of the family may have helped out. His letter suggests that the family did pay for themselves, but there is some evidence that a 'gentleman' had advanced money for P.E.C emigrants in 1832 and 1833 in the Billingshurst area[11] and it is possible he helped again with the Voice family's expenses.

The Fifth Duke of Richmond at Goodwood House was the authority to whom Sockett turned when he needed administrative help. The Fourth Duke had been Governor General of Canada from 1818-1819. By 1834 the Fifth Duke was 43. He was Postmaster General in the Whig Reform Ministry of 1830 during his short secession from the Tory party. He was Colonel of the Sussex Militia and Vice-Admiral of Sussex, and had been a government appointed Commissioner of Emigration between 1831 and 1832. He was described as having 'a certain measure of understanding' and as 'prejudiced, narrow-minded, illiterate, and ignorant, good -looking , good- humoured and unaffected, tedious, prolix, unassuming, and a duke'! In May 1830 he asked Parliament for a select committee to be appointed to consider the internal state of the country 'particularly with respect to the working classes' a request that was overwhelmingly defeated. In November of the same year he was reputed to have done battle against a band of two hundred labourers , during the agricultural 'swing' riots, whom he beat with the help of fifty of his tenant farmers. He was said to have then harangued the rioters, sending them away in 'good humour'. He had an aptitude and liking for cricket, a pleasure he shared with Cornelius Voice and his sons.[12] William Cobbett, the radical journalist, was in turn to harangue Richmond over his less than good humoured implementation of the regulations of the 1834 Poor Law Amendment Act in Richmond's neighbourhood of West Sussex. Sockett wrote regularly to Richmond during the two months before the *British Tar* sailed giving details of the progress of the preparations and asking for help over such problems as emigration tax, and the fraught question of the Superintendent Surgeon, a new appointee for this ship, James Marr Brydone.

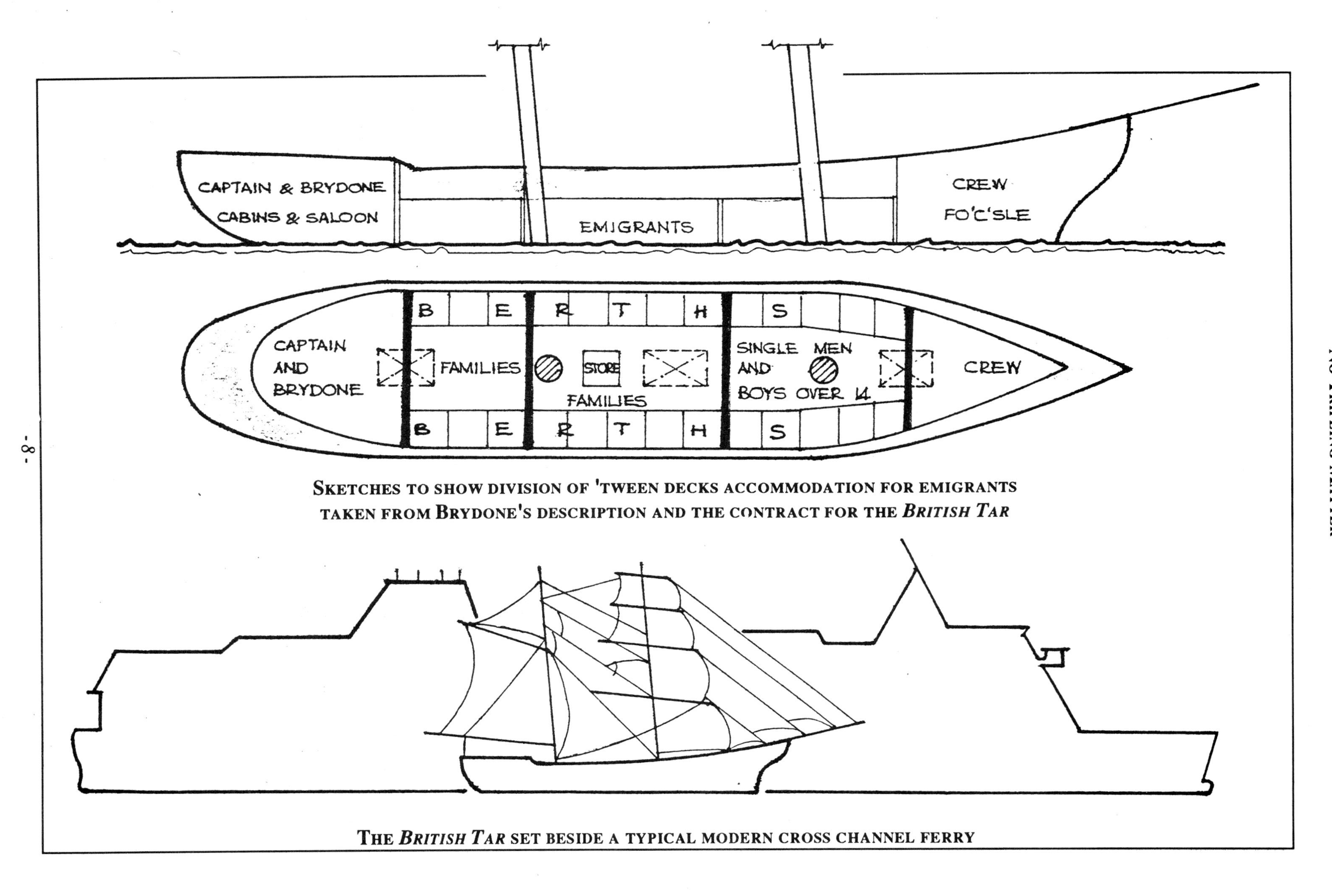

SKETCHES TO SHOW DIVISION OF 'TWEEN DECKS ACCOMMODATION FOR EMIGRANTS TAKEN FROM BRYDONE'S DESCRIPTION AND THE CONTRACT FOR THE *BRITISH TAR*

THE *BRITISH TAR* SET BESIDE A TYPICAL MODERN CROSS CHANNEL FERRY

3:THE *BRITISH TAR*

Waiting at the quayside at Portsmouth was the *British Tar*, A1, 383 tons register, built in Sunderland in 1824. She was owned by Forrest, her captain was Master Robert Crawford and she had been commissioned from Carter and Bonus, shipping agents of Leadenhall Street London, who handled many emigrant ships.The crew on ships of this size usually numbered 20 or less. The agreement between the P.E.C. and Carter and Bonus[13] stated that the ship was to proceed from London to Portsmouth harbour on or before 5 April 1834, there to receive on board from 12 April onwards her passengers, together with their stores, provisions, baggage, and furniture - if Hale's advice had been heeded there would not be too much of the latter!

The ship had been fitted up in a 'substantial manner' with a double row of berths, each six feet square, running each side of the whole length of the between - decks of the ship from the bulkhead of the Captain's cabin to that which bounded the seamen's quarters.

A partition was built across this central area before the main hatchway and another abaft the main mast by which the emigrants' quarters were divided into three parts. Each part had its own separate access, that is by the fore, main and aft hatchways. The division forward was to be the quarters of the boys and single men above 14 years of age. The other two divisions were given to families and single women. On the *British Tar* these two groups seem to have been mixed together, whereas on some emigrant ships the families took the middle section and the young women were separated into the further third division. The contract also stipulated that there was to be one water closet between decks, but the Superintendent, Brydone, said in his log that there were two, [14] one for each of the families' and women's sections; a true convenience for them,although there would have been at least fifty people using these two lavatories. The confined conditions on the *British Tar* might be likened to those encountered on a package transatlantic flight today, but the emigrants counted their travelling time in weeks rather than hours. They could, of course, escape on deck when the weather permitted and indeed the young men had to do so, whatever the weather, for their lavatory was there. A store-room was erected between decks and a water cistern. Two cooking hearths were provided for the passengers, and another for the ship's crew, plus sufficient coal for cooking. Forty tons of 'good sweet water' in proper casks were put on board for the passengers' sole use.

No passengers were permitted on board without the consent of the P.E.C. The Master, at the risk of a £50 fine, was to ensure that no liquor or other articles were sold on board without the consent of the Superintendent. The Superintendent's control over alcohol seems to have been a constant source of irritation on several P.E.C. voyages. The Master was not permitted to bring back to England any of the emigrants sent out by the P.E.C. under a penalty of £10 for anyone so returned. Presumably, the Committee did not wish to see the swift return of their assisted emigrants, especially defaulting parents.

Carter and Bonus were to be paid £400 for up to 100 passages, children under 14 being calculated as a half passage and infants under one year not counting at all. Any passengers over the 100 limit were to be paid for at the rate of £3 per head with children in the same proportion as before.The *British Tar* sailed with 135 passengers, 81 men, 20 women and 34 children so the P.E.C. had to pay some excess fares above the £400. Carter and Bonus were to receive two thirds of the total sum when the *British Tar* cleared Portsmouth and the rest when they had completed the contract. The agreement also contained clauses stipulating that if the ship was delayed in sailing by the owners, or the Captain, then the passengers were to be fed during the delay by the owners of the ship. If the P.E.C. held up departure then they would pay a penalty of £9 per day to the owners and feed the emigrants themselves. These latter stipulations were some credit to the P.E.C. for many emigrants going independently on purely commercially operated ships were greatly impoverished if their departure was held up for any reason and they had to pay for sometimes lengthy stays in lodgings at the port of departure.

Brydone, as the Surgeon Superintendent on the voyage, was to have a cabin of his own and was to take charge of the medicine chest until the ship reached Montreal, when it was to be handed over to Captain Crawford and brought back to England for return to Petworth.

4:MEDICINES FOR BODY AND SOUL

This medicine chest and a load of books were two particular items of cargo stowed on board for the passengers' physical and spiritual welfare. The provision of a surgeon and a medicine chest on emigrant ships was a variable and ill- enforced legal requirement in the first half of the 19th century. Emigrant ships to North America were not required by law to carry a surgeon. Nevertheless, Carter and Bonus usually ensured that one was sent on their ships and the P.E.C supported this policy, although Sockett had written earlier to the Colonial Office complaining of the 'expensiveness and inconvenience' of providing a surgeon and medicine chest.[15] We do not know what Brydone was paid as surgeon on the *British Tar*. In 1839, Mr.Ryan, the surgeon on the *Waterloo*, a P.E.C. supervised ship from Ireland, was paid £50. This, with the cost of the medicine chest, £5 2s.10d. in the case of the *British Tar*, would have meant an expense of about 8s. per person on the latter ship. Brydone may well have received more than £50 for he had onerous duties as Superintendent of the party in addition to his medical responsibilities.

Brydone was held in high regard by Sockett, but the presence of a surgeon on board ship did not automatically ensure a high standard of medical care. Surgeons were not the elite of the medical profession in the 19th century and a ship's surgeon came low in status in an already lowly profession.

In March 1834 Sockett purchased the medical supplies for the *British Tar* from Thomas Hodgkinson & Co. Snow Hill London. The predominant categories of disease and distress to be treated were coughs, colds and chest infections; stomach upsets including, of course, sea sickness; wounds of varying degrees; conditions calling for stimulants or carminatives; fevers; skin infections and parasites. The favourite cure-all of the surgeon seemed to be Magnesium Sulphate, or Epsom salts, for the *British Tar* medicine chest contained 18 lbs. of this and Brydone was to use 8 lbs.on the voyage. He also had the equipment to make his own pills and draughts, and stocks of vinegar, mustard, soap, preserved meat and porter that he could dispense to the needy and sick.

Publishers and booksellers were increasingly moving into the rapidly expanding market of emigrant literature. J. Phillips, the Petworth printers and publishers ,who produced the P.E.C. literature and posters, advertised a number of publications offering helpful information and advice, ranging from McGregor's *British America*, 2 vols., at £1.8s. through *Statistical Sketches of Upper Canada by a Backwoodsman* at 1s.6d., to Hale's book at 2d., or 1s.6d. a dozen copies.

The Society for Promoting Christian Knowledge, the Church of England publishing house, gave a grant of their books worth £25 for the use of the passengers on the *British Tar*. Egremont subscribed £20 annually to the S.P.C.K. and the Bishop and Dean of Chichester were prominent members of S.P.C.K. Committees. Dr. Chandler, the Dean, wrote to the S.P.C.K. in London in April 1834 asking for a grant of Bibles and other religious books for emigrants 'about to proceed to Canada under the superintendence of the Rev. T. Sockett'. [16] The ensuing grant of £25 was a relatively generous one, and the S.P.C.K. was to give the same to later P.E.C. ships. Much of this grant was in the form of Bibles, Prayer Books and Testaments. Each emigrant was given a Bible, and Brydone later distributed New Testaments to people he met in Canada. It is not recorded what other books were in the 1834 cargo but by 1839, at the suggestion of William Gladstone, then Parliamentary Under-Secretary to the Colonial Secretary, the S.P.C.K. had put together a standard *Emigrants Library* drawn from its existing catalogue. The Committee wrote of the need for this enterprise;

It is fearful to contemplate the growth of states, such as we are founding both in North America and the Australian dominions, likely to lead to such a height of physical well-being, in conjunction with so great a degree of religious destitution.[17]

The *Emigrants Library* to mitigate such religious destitution consisted almost wholly of theological and highly moral works ranging from Paley's *Natural Theology* and *Sermon on the Terrors of the Lord*, Blunt's *History of the Reformation*, and *Learn to Die* by Christopher Sutton, to *Simple Stories for Cottagers' Children.*

Brydone later reported to Sockett that the *British Tar* passengers had found the S.P.C.K. books 'particularly acceptable and useful'. [18] How useful they were in a spiritual sense one does not know. Certainly, *Narratives of the Shipwrecks of the Lady Hobart Packet, Cabalva, Centaur and Lichfield* might have induced a properly serious spiritual state of mind in the travellers. However, Samuel Richardson seems to have had doubts over 'usefulness' very early on for he sold his Bible for 1s.6d. to a fellow emigrant from Hellingly before they reached Portsmouth. Perhaps he could not read, perhaps he needed the 1s 6d. more. Samuel was later given a replacement Bible by Brydone with 'advice and admonition' at a public ceremony on shipboard.[19]

The S.P.C.K. books contained little of practical use, although *Simple Stories for Cottagers' Children*, if it was included in the package, may well have helped to entertain the children who were ill at sea. By 1838 the *Emigrants Library* was to contain one practically useful book, *The Instructor*, which in Vol.11 dealt with The House, Material Used in Building, Furniture, Food and Clothing, and this series was later enlarged to three more Volumes dealing with The Universe, The Natural World, The Human Form, Lessons on Health, Descriptive Geography and a detailed calendar.

In January 1835,as an expression of the P.E.C.'s thanks, Sockett presented the S.P.C.K. Committee with a copy of the newly published *Narrative of a Voyage with a Party of Emigrants Sent Out from Sussex in 1834...* by Brydone.

The passengers, their luggage, the provisions, the water, the coal for cooking, the medicines and the books were finally stowed on board and on the 17 April Sockett wrote to Richmond, 'I have much pleasure in stating that the ship was out of sight with a leading breeze to take her through the Needles at ten minutes after 4 this afternoon. The people highly satisfied and in excellent spirits.'[20]

AT SEA

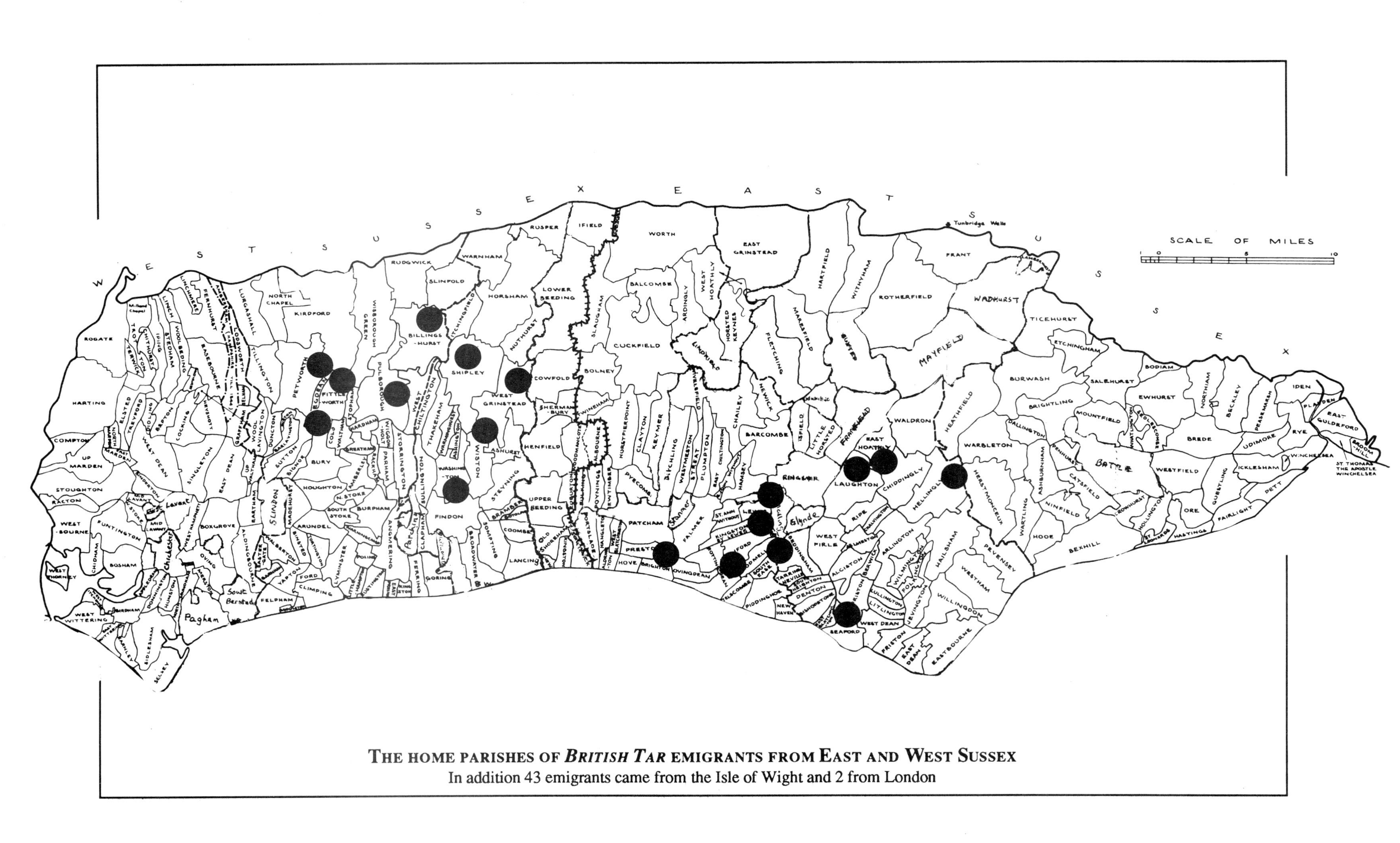

The home parishes of *British Tar* emigrants from East and West Sussex

In addition 43 emigrants came from the Isle of Wight and 2 from London

1:THE PASSENGERS

In riding once, about five years ago, from Petworth to Horsham, on a Sunday in the afternoon, I came to a solitary cottage, which stood at about twenty yards distance from the road. There was the wife with the baby in her arms, the husband teaching another child to walk, while four more were at play before them. I stopped and looked at them for some time, and then, turning my horse, rode up to the wicket, getting into talk by asking the distance to Horsham. I found that the man worked chiefly in the woods, and that he was doing pretty well. The wife was then only twenty two, and the man only twenty five. She was a pretty woman, even for Sussex, which, not excepting Lancashire, contains the prettiest women in England. He was a very fine and stout young man. 'Why', said I, 'how many children do you reckon to have at last?' 'I do not care how many,' said the man: 'God never sends mouths without sending meat.' 'Did you ever hear,' said I, 'of one Parson Malthus?' 'No, sir.' 'Why, if he were to hear of your works, he would be outrageous; for he wants an Act of Parliament to prevent poor people from marrying young, and from having such lots of children.' 'Oh! the brute!' exclaimed the wife; while the husband laughed, thinking that I was joking. I asked the man whether he had ever had relief from the parish; and upon his answering in the negative, I took out my purse, took from it enough to bait my horse at Horsham, and to clear my turnpikes to Worth, whither I was going to stay awhile, and gave him all the rest. Now, is it not a shame, is it not a sin of all sins, that people like these should, by acts of the Government, be reduced to such misery as to be induced to abandon their homes and their country, to seek, in a foreign land, the means of preventing themselves and their children from starving ? And this had been, and now is, actually the case with many such families in this same county of Sussex!

William Cobbett, *Advice to Young Men* , 1824, Advice to a Lover.

As they left their home and their country for a foreign land, whom did Elizabeth and Cornelius Voice find as fellow travellers and families in the steerage of the *British Tar*? Amongst the relatively few from Petworth and its surrounding district there were three Uptons from Petworth itself - Frederick Upton, aged 24, his younger brother a boy called Egbert, and a cousin. They were going to join William and Clifford Upton who had sailed with the P.E.C. scheme in 1832. William had sent back enthusiastic accounts of opportunities in Canada. He was working at a sawmill for 12s.6d. a week plus board and lodging and wrote 'Give my love to all my brothers and sisters, tell them ... if they cannot get a living in England, to come to Canada where they may soon get an independency.' [21] Another young boy, George Sheppard, came from nearby Egdean. The Earl of Egremont probably paid his passage and Egdean Vestry fitted him out for the voyage with £5.0.5d.worth of clothes. The Reverend J.K.Greetham, from nearby Kirdford, who had shepherded a party of parishioners onto the *Lord Melville* and the *Eveline* in 1832, escorted George to Portsmouth. George had had one shilling to spend en-route, presumably on refreshment, and Mr Greetham furnished him with £3.19.5d.worth of cash and goods - probably his bedding and eating irons - chargeable to Egdean parish, before he embarked.[22]

William Green, his wife and three children, came from Pulborough. William had been a Serjeant of the 36th regiment and, as an army man, was entitled to a government grant of 200 acres of land in Canada. William seems to have fallen on hard times for Pulborough Vestry minutes record on 14 March 1834 that 'William Green was to be sent to Canada' and he was ordered to see Mr Sockett. On 26 March William applied for assistance to enable him to go to Canada. It is not clear if the Vestry paid for his passage but they certainly voted money to transport him and his family to Portsmouth and granted him £5 to be shared amongst the whole family for clothes. Brydone reckoned that men like William Green were exactly the kind of emigrants that Canada needed. 'There are no men more accustomed to hardship and fatigue; none are better suited to become useful settlers, than officers of the navy and army. No men better calculated to preserve regularity and order...'[23] Brydone was to employ William Green's talents for keeping order on board ship.

A considerable number of people came from East Sussex. Fifty seven emigrants from the Brighton and Lewes area had arrived at Portsmouth and been safely stowed on board by 15 April. An Emigration Committee of the large landowners and magistrates of East Sussex had been set up at the end of 1833. The Earl of Chichester, at Stanmer, headed this Committee and appealed to local philanthropic and parish authorities to support the funding of emigration.(24) Henry Harwood, a shoemaker from Lewes, was emigrating with three of his grown-up sons, Henry, Alfred and Richard. They had been sponsored by Mr Hurly, a Lewes banker, and Mr Rogers of Southover.(25) Hurly lived at Iford where Henry and his wife Sarah had been married in 181O, so there was perhaps some long-standing link between the two. Sarah had died in 1818, soon after Richard was born. Abraham Muzzall came from Brighton. He was single,aged 20, and, like Cornelius Voice, a carpenter and a chapel man. He was a member of Salem Particular Baptist Chapel in Bond Street, Brighton.(26)

Other East Sussex emigrants came from outlying villages. Mary and William West had lived in East Hoathly. Mary West was 32. Married at 18, when she embarked she had seven children ranging from Mary, aged 12, to Francis who was 15 months. She was now seven months pregnant with her eighth child. She was not alone in her pregnancy for at least two other women were also pregnant, one, Mrs Ditton,very much so. It was no rare thing for women to set sail in the last stages of pregnancy. Two babies were born on the *England* the year before, and others were to arrive on later P.E.C. ships. Mary's husband, William, was 41. He had been christened in December 1792 as the 'base-born' son of Sarah West, a pauper. He appears in East Hoathly parish records as William Warden, alias West. When William was five, his mother had married Charles Warden. Warden may have been William's real father, or his step-father. Nevertheless, William would always officially remain 'base-born', bearing his mother's maiden name.

In the years before 1834 Mary and her husband both applied regularly for relief from the Poor Law Overseers. In January 1833, for example, after the birth of Francis, Mary was granted five gallons of flour. She said her husband could not earn enough to support his family. In the summer of the same year she asked again for relief and was left to the 'discretion of one of the overseers'. William also made intermittent appeals to the parish. One was for a nurse for his wife after Francis was born, and for a handbill and gloves - presumably equipment for hedging or coppicing. He was granted 5s.on this occasion. A vivid insight into the family's plight was given in October 1832 when William was granted 5s.to mend his windows before the winter. A glimpse of the general unemployment and distress in East Hoathly in the winter of 1833/34 is to be found in the Vestry minute for December 1833 in which a Vestry member, Mr Gardiner, proposed an extra rate to be taken up to form a fund to find work for unemployed labourers, a suggestion which was approved, and then squashed as unlawful by Chichester's steward. Chichester owned considerable land in East Hoathly.

In January 1834, after further unsuccessful appeals for help, one of the West sons was granted a pair of boots and there was a minute noting that the parish would pay half the expenses of sending William Warden, alias West, and his family to Canada along with another East Hoathly family, the Hutsons. By February William was said to be 'willing to emigrate' but needed relief for the present; he was granted six gallons of flour.

East Hoathly apparently paid their half of the expense of sending the Wests by raising a loan from Mr Smith of Lewes, to be repaid in four annual instalments. Chichester possibly, or probably, paid the rest. The Parish also contracted to pay £12.1Os.toward the expenses of William Hutson, his wife and four sons. Under the P.E.C. their fare would have been at least £4O. The Hutsons do not appear by name in any of the *British Tar* archives so we have no record as to whether they did in fact embark. There is no mention in the East Hoathly parish records of any £5 clothing or equipment for these emigrants.(27) The West family were possibly very ill-equipped for their immediate and long-term future; on the other hand their struggle for survival in East Hoathly may have made them very sturdy and appreciative first generation Canadians. One interesting sidelight on the Wests' economic plight might be observed in Brydone's later remark that William West was 'an old smuggler'.(28) By the 183Os the authorities were clamping down hard on smuggling in Sussex and a useful, probably vital, supplement to a family income - literally moonlighting - was becoming scarce and hazardous.

From the neighbouring parish of Hellingly eight single men had been sent; John Barton, Peter Pelling, John Tutt, James Parsons, William Ripley, Samuel Richardson and two Hammonds - Edward and Henry.(29) The two Hammonds were possibly brothers and, like William West, 'base-born'. Both of them were labourers who had received intermittent payments for parish labour in 1832 and 1833. Single unemployed labourers, very often men stood off by the farmer at the beginning of winter, would be set to work by the parish if at all possible, and paid around 4s.a week. If no work was available they might be granted outdoor relief of the same sum. Samuel Richardson and James Tutt had also received this kind of parish relief. James Tutt asked for his last week's pay as he set off for Canada, a request that was refused. Hellingly Vestry did agree, though, to give the suggested £5 per head for equipping their emigrants. The two Hammonds, Samuel Richardson and John Barton also received a few shillings relief in the days before their departure for 'needs'. The Vestry also paid the men's travelling expenses to Lewes, where they were, presumably, to join the main East Sussex party. The men asked for 5s.but were given 3s. As we have seen,Samuel Richardson re-couped some of his shortfall by selling his Bible. Hellingly Vestry paid half of the emigrants' expenses by a loan funded by Chichester, who again owned land in the parish and was patron of the parish church, and Thomas Calverly, of Ewell Castle in Surrey,another Hellingly landowner.

Forty three people went from the Isle of Wight,amongst them thirty paupers from the House of Industry,the joint workhouse for all the Island's parishes.This workhouse had room for 920 people. In 1831 the Governor of the House reported that there were 500 children in residence.(30) It cost 4s.5d.per week to keep each pauper. In 1834 there were also 322 families receiving out-door relief of money or bread, and many labourers were being employed on parish work either at road making or spade husbandry schemes - using labour intensive hand digging rather than the plough.

The House of Industry authorities used emigration for some years as one means of reducing their pauper population. Twenty-nine tradesmen and labourers went from Cowes to New York in 1831 (31) and from 1832 onwards, when the P.E.C. was at work, the authorities regularly despatched emigrants on their ships, sometimes negotiating cut price rates for large numbers. In April 1834 the Governor was granted £500 for his emigration funds.(32) This would have allowed the *British Tar* emigrants £10 for their passage, £5 for clothes and equipment - they were said to be fitted out with 'care and attention'- (33) and £50 over for the cost of sending the party to Portsmouth and any other incidental expenses. Not all of this £50 may have been spent on the *British Tar* emigrants, however, for other paupers were being sent on other ships in the spring and summer of 1834.

There is no list of these thirty men, women and youngsters sent on the *British Tar*. We know the name of only one, William Squibb, and have made guesses that other passengers, whose names we know, came from the Island. Although the authorities claimed in the press in 1834 that they sent the 'healthyest and most industrious'(34) the Governor admitted in 1831 that he would most like to send away the 'lazy the idle and the dissolute'(35). If he succeeded in doing so goes unrecorded, but certainly in 1837 the Captain of the P.E.C. ship the *Diana* spoke in very unflattering terms of his passengers from the Isle of Wight as troublemakers.(36) The men and women themselves might have told a different story. One man, Job Hodge, a passenger on the *British Tar* and most probably from the Island, had a melancholy history as a poor labourer. His eldest son had died at birth. His wife, Jane, died in the House of Industry in November 1833, and Francis, Job's youngest son, was buried in May 1834 aged 14 months, in the same place, a few weeks after his father had been sent away to Canada.(37) It would seem small wonder that this little Francis died, for a coroner's inquest and investigation into conditions in The House of Industry in June 1834 found that 46 bedsteads had been crammed into a small garrett, 'wretchedly ventilated'. Sixty children slept in the 46 beds, each of which had been shortened to four feet four inches to allow passage up the room. The children were shut overnight into this room which was like an oven by morning.(38) Emigrants coming from conditions such as these must have found the cramped conditions on the *British Tar* relatively spacious and agreeable.

Some of the emigrants from the Isle of Wight were young boys. They, with George Sheppard and others, made up a party of unaccompanied youngsters that were put under Brydone's especial charge and were to be apprenticed out by him on their arrival in Canada.

Disbursments to the Poor of
1834 the Parish of Egdean

18 — Mr Greetham for Cash & Goods furnished to George Sheppard, at Portsmouth on his embarking for Canada — 3 19 5
— Cash to G. Sheppard on Road — 1 0

THE SHIP

BRITISH TAR,

A 1. coppered and copper fastened,

Burthen 383 Tons per Resister,

is engaged by the PETWORTH EMIGRATION COMMITTEE,

to sail from

PORTSMOUTH

FOR

MONTREAL, DIRECT,

On THURSDAY, the 17th. of APRIL next,

(Passengers must be on board before 6 in the Evening of Tuesday, the 15th, or at latest by Noon on Wednesday, the 16th.)

with Emigrants from different parts of the County of SUSSEX.

The Committee have much pleasure in stating, that they have prevailed on a Gentleman of high respectability, a SURGEON of nearly 30 years standing in the Navy, and whose practice has been considerable, both on shore and afloat, to take the entire charge of the Emigrants who go out in the BRITISH TAR. He will have the controul of all the arrangements to YORK, Upper Canada, (or to any other Port at the head of *Lake Ontario*); and though he will not be authorized on the part of the Committee, to incur any expences for Conveyance, *&c.* beyond the head of the Lake, yet he will, with the assistance of the Government Agents, use his best endeavours towards forwarding the different Parties to those places where they have Friends already settled, or to which they may wish to proceed, and also in finding Employment for those who have no particular engagements.

A large number of Passages being already engaged on board this Ship, applications must be made as early as possible to Mr. J. PHILLIPS, Petworth; of whom, or of Mr. KENNARD, 20, Penny Street, Portsmouth, further Information may be obtained.

A few Cabin Passengers could be accommodated, and Berths may be secured in the intermediate Cabin, at a small advance on the Steerage price.

Petworth, March 22nd. 1834.

J. Phillips, Printer, Petworth.

2: MORAL HEALTH AND WELFARE

Given the diverse background of her passengers, and some bad publicity about conduct on the *England* in 1833, Sockett was anxious that the *British Tar* should be known as a respectable ship. A month before she sailed the P.E.C. still had appointed no Surgeon Superintendent. Sockett wrote to Richmond on 18 March 1834:

My Lord Duke

*We **have engaged** The British Tar, a highly proper vessel for the purpose,to sail from Portsmouth for Montreal on the 17th April, and are anxious to put forth a bill, **fully** detailing **all** the advantages we are able to offer on board her, but are preventedfrom doing so,for the present, on account of not being able to compleat our arrangements, as to Surgeon and Superintendent,...*

*I am very desirous to send Mr Brydone; as his taking the charge would give great eclat to the expedition; probably induce several to come forward who would not otherwise do so, and set **us** at ease about drunkeness and peculation..*

*In the meanwhile, **the day of sailing approaches** and **some** arrangements **must** be made, and givenforth to the public...*

Some of the emigrants going out on our ship are very respectable, I am therefore, the more anxious to provide handsomely for them...[39]

Sockett's anxiety about drunkeness and peculation was understandable as there had been disturbing accusations published in the Canadian and British press of shady practice and drunkeness on the part of the Superintendent of the *England*, Captain Hale, in the previous year. The reputation of Egremont, and Sockett as Rector of Petworth, was also at stake and the work of the P.E.C. was likely to be curtailed if their ships regularly had a bad name. The reputation of emigrant ships was dubious at the best of times, with reports circulating of overcrowding, close confinement with all kinds of men, women, and children in foetid holds, bad food and water, sickness and disease, drunkeness and sexual licence.

Sockett regarded Brydone as 'from education; habits; and situation; of quite a different class from those who have heretofore gone out as Superintendents.'[40] James Marr Brydone, a Scotsman of 55, had been a naval surgeon for many years. This was his first journey for the P.E.C.

and he was to superintend their next three ships. He had earlier in his career taken a party of convicts to Australia. Sockett doubtless valued his experience for he wrote with evident relief to Richmond on 22 March

I am much pleased at being able to inform you that Mr. Brydone takes the charge of our emigrants- a fact which was no sooner known than it decided three doubtful ones, and the public announcement of which,will, I doubt not, produce a considerable effect next week.

I send some of our large bills, and have the honour to be etc.[42]

These large posters, made much of the fact of Brydone's presence on the *British Tar*: 'The Committee have much pleasure in stating that they have prevailed on a Gentleman of high respectability, a surgeon of nearly 30 years standing in the Navy and whose practice has been considerable, both on shore and afloat to take the entire charge of the Emigrants'

How much Brydone tempered his discipline for these emigrants from that he had imposed on the convicts we do not know. He, too, was to come under attack in 1837 for harsh aggressive behaviour on the *Diana*, an accusation[43] that was firmly refuted. He certainly lost no time in imposing order and regulation on the *British Tar*.

The day after we left Spithead I formed the annexed Scale of daily Rations and the subsequent day the following Rules and Regulations that every man might know what he had to expect and what was required of him:

***First:** Bread and Water will be issued every morning between six and seven. Meat and Potatoes at Ten in the Forenoon on Sundays, Tuesdays, Thursdays, and Saturdays. And on these days Brandy, or Rum and Water, at two in the afternoon.*

***Second:** Flour, Cheese, Butter and Raisins on Monday, Wednesday, and Fridays at Ten in the forenoon- Tea and Sugar on Saturdays at Four in the afternoon.*

***Third:** One man to be selected from each Mess to draw the provisions. J. Gamblin, W. Green and W. Martin in daily rotation the issuing of the Provisions and Water etc. to see that the Messes occasion no delay and that justice is done to all.*

***Fourth:** The Heads of the Messes in the Fore-Steerage; C. Voice, J. Perring; H. Snelling, and W.Warren ;in the Middle-Steerage; J.Bassam,George Coleman,Thos Ditton; and W. West in the After-Steerage to see that the Berths and Deck of the [ship] be properly cleaned every Morning before Nine. The Deck swept after every meal the Water Cistern kept constantly supplied with Water by the Young Men in rotation who are requested also to give some assistance to the families if required by the Superintendent.*

***Fifth:** J. Gamblin, W. Green and W. Martin to inspect the Berths daily and report to the Superintendent prior to his inspection in the forenoon.*

***Sixth:** All the Parties before named to prevent smoaking [sic] between decks, swearing or improper conduct of any sort and all are requested to refrain from such acts as disturb the Peace Comfort and harmony of the whole.*

***Seventh:** No person to take or remove a Light from the Lamps or Move the Lamps from their position unless directed by the Superintendent or Master of the Ship*

***Eighth:** All complaints or cause of Complaint to be submitted to the Superintendent who will immediately inquire into them and as far as in his power cause them to be removed.*

By uniform regularity in issuing the provisions, a strict observance of the Rules and Regulations and by appointing Four of the Young men in rotation daily to assist the Cook in getting up Coals and Water to keep the Upper Deck clean and dry and to fill the Water Cistern all have been contented and I have comparatively speaking experienced very little trouble[44]

The regulations certainly smack of a well disciplined naval regime. As well as rules and regulations though, Brydone seems to have used discreet bribery to good effect. As guardian of the liquor supply he was generous with the 'Eau de Vie'. He rewarded Frederick Upton, John Gamblin, William Green and William Martin with a bottle of brandy each week for their supervisory duties, and gave a bottle of rum weekly to the cook and the men who had assisted him and, 'thought it advisable to give also a Bottle weekly to the Ships Company in order to promote a good understanding between them and the people'[45] In addition all the passengers got a ration of rum, or brandy, diluted with water, four times a week. They might well also have had their own extra supplies prudently hidden amongst their luggage.

The charge to prevent smoking between decks was largely a matter of fire hazard on a wooden ship, although smoking in the steerage would have heightened the foul atmosphere created by mass feeding, meagre sanitation, and sickness. Swearing had been tackled by Hale in his *Instructions to Emigrants*; ' let it be your pride, that your conduct shall be that of a sober and respectable man; Let your example to your children, be, such as a father's should be never swearing yourself nor allowing it in them, but correct them severely, and promptly, if they should attain that vice.' The children would probably attain a great deal from the ship's crew, if not from other passengers, and would need a considerable amount of correction. The clause about not disturbing the comfort and harmony of 'the whole' probably sprang from an incident on the *England*. Hale had reported in his log that the single men became 'turbulent and refractory' refusing to put out their lights at a proper time at night and disturbing the rest of the ship by playing cards and gambling. [46] On the other hand, the young men were doubtless only too glad to be separated from the crying babies and noisy fretful children.

The moral respectability of emigrant ships was maintained, at least in theory, by the practice of separating the young and single men from the young women and families. The elder Voice sons would, therefore, have berths in the forecastle section of the steerage with the Hammonds, the Harwoods, Abraham Muzzall and the other single men. Elizabeth and Cornelius Voice with young Elizabeth, Martha, George and Joseph would have berths in one of the family sections. They would, as a family, be entitled to one and a half six feet square berths. Mary and William West with their seven children under 14 would have been entitled to five and a half sleeping places; the child in the womb would perhaps have been taken into consideration and ensured the family two six feet square berths for their own use. William West was head of the Mess in the after-steerage presumably where his family was lodged.

The lack of privacy may well have given Elizabeth Voice, her daughters, and all the women in the family sections considerable concern. A contemporary traveller on another emigrant ship to America described how 'many decent females, who had been accustomed to comforts in their homes, burst into tears to find they must dress and undress partially when exposed to the eyes of strangers, perhaps of the other sex'[47] The passengers would probably have rigged up rough curtains around their berths if they were lucky enough to have one for their own family group. William Cobbett in his *Emigrants Guide*, (1829),gave practical advice on how women could dress and undress in the steerage with due modesty. They were especially advised to have dresses with front fastenings for ease of dressing in a small space.

On Sundays the spiritual welfare of the passengers was catered for by a service on deck when Brydone read prayers, and on the first Sunday out, a sermon that Sockett had written in 1832 for the emigrants on board the *Eveline* and *Lord Melville*. Brydone doubtless felt that Sockett would be gratified to hear that it was 'pleasing to see,the very respectable appearance made by the emigrants, in the neatness and cleanliness of their dress, when they came on deck, to attend the service of the church on sundays...'[48]

In a more secular mood the morale of the ship's company was kept up after a long spell of rough weather and sea-sickness by some fun. On the 15 May, two days after the passengers had first sighted land and a remarkable fine day, the people were enjoying themselves on deck dancing to the violin. A fiddle player was always welcome on board ship. Many emigrants throughout the 19th century testified to the pleasure of singing and dancing to the violin. Dancing also offered good exercise in a restricted space, a welcome antidote to the acute confinement below deck. Some of the *British Tar* passengers were evidently good singers, for some weeks later when they were settling in Blandford they told Brydone of the ceremony of the opening of their new church; 'We conducted the singing; and you would have liked to have heard us'.[49]

3: PHYSICAL HEALTH AND WELFARE

Physical conditions on the *British Tar* were betterthan those on many emigrant ships. Sockett maintained that economy should not be the overriding factor, these emigrants were to be treated humanely for they were not 'soldiers and sailors, accustomed to be closely stowed on board ship; but ... country women, and helpless children, of all ages, who have been bred up in the enjoyment of free space, and fresh air.' [50] This last was not wholly true of conditions inside many labourers' cottages which were often small and crammed with large families, but there was certainly space and fresh air outside - the Wests probably had more than enough fresh air inside too with their erstwhile broken windows.

The Passenger Act of 1828 allowed emigrant ships to carry three adults for every four tons register, children under 14 counting as half a passage. *The British Tar*, 383 tons, could, therefore legally have taken 287 passages including the crew. In fact she only carried at most 118 passages plus the crew. That is, 81 men and 20 women; 101 full passages plus 34 children; 17 passages. If any of the children were under oneyear old they did not count at all so the number of actual passages may have been even less. The crew certainly did not number 169. The ship may not have been as full as the P.E.C. wished, for on the *England* (384 tons) in 1833 they had put 166 passages. Some emigrant ships crammed people on by putting a further row of berths down the centre of the steerage, blocking the central passageway leaving no gangway and no space for tables at which passengers could sit and eat.

Sockett does admit that concern for the emigrants was not totally on their behalf; 'Policy would dictate this; for sad accounts sent back, of the miseries of the voyage, will deter numbers from venturing upon it ... a most powerful check to future emigration; especially from the neighbourhood whence the sufferers had gone.'[51]

Many owners of emigrant ships required steerage passengers to take their own food which was often stored along with other luggage around or within the passenger's berth. The *British Tar* supplied provisions and a storage room for luggage.

To modern sensibilities two water closets were woefully few for the use of all the married couples and children. Such lack of amenities could have caused much distress especially when sea-sickness struck. After ten days at sea one w.c. was damaged by a large bone stuck in a leaden pipe. The ship's carpenter made a hash of mending it injuring the pipe so much it had to be removed. It was eventually repaired by two emigrants, Henry Kemp and another young Kemp. This careless misuse of the w.c. could well have arisen from sheer ignorance, for many of the rural passengers would not have been familiar with such formal conveniences.

Cleanliness of the ship and the passengers was one of Brydone's chief concerns. The heads of the messes were deputed to see that the steerage was cleaned every morning before Brydone made a tour of inspection. Hale, in his pamphlet, laid great stress on cleanliness too, although he did feel that as English families the emigrants were at an advantage: 'Fortunate it is for a man at sea, with his family, that he has an English wife, with whom cleanliness is a predominant virtue.' The implied unfortunate man in Hale's opinion was probably Irish. Hale advised the voyagers to wash regularly with salt water, and urged parents to bath their children daily using the large tub provided for scrubbing the deck. He admitted that the 'small fry' could be troublesome over this cold bath and suggested bribing them with gingerbread. William Cobbett, a firm advocate of cold baths for infants at all times, admitted the practice entailed a struggle; he recommended that the parent sing more loudly and persistently than the child could scream.[52] Lice were a perpetual problem. Hale insisted that attention to cleanliness between decks would reduce the scourge, and regular combing of the childrens' heads should help to keep them free of nits.

Laundry was a hard task. Clothes had to be washed in salt water, and lines of dripping garments suspended (if the necessary lines and hooks had been thoughtfully taken on board) on wet days within the steerage, or strung up on deck when weather permitted. In such conditions the garments would hardly ever be totally dry and the salt water would foster skin complaints. Hale advised that a little fresh water would be a boon for washing the children's clothes if some could be saved out of the family's daily allowance. How did the mothers of small infants cope, did they take a supply of disposable rags?. Certainly older emigrants were advised by earlier travellers to wear their oldest clothes and shoes on board ship. The *British Tar* people were to be glad of their warm clothing when they reached the Newfoundland banks and saw the icebergs; on 8 May the temperature reached only 31 degrees fahrenheit, a degree below freezing.

Keeping the children amused in such limited space was a real problem. Advantage had to be seized of any opportunity to send them on deck to run off surplus energy. Hale suggested that older children could help to clean the berth space and also assist the sailors scrubbing the decks. We are not told what the sailors thought about this voluntary assistance, but Brydone's discreet bribing with the extra bottle of rum to the crew seems to have produced an amicable situation, for Brydone said he had no complaints. Encouraging the children to run around on deck, however, was not without its problems, they needed constant watching, for instance, to see that they did not fall through the open hatches. Nevertheless, Robert Louis Stevenson, sailing on an emigrant ship some forty years later, said that the children were the first to settle down on shipboard as they climbed about the deck and into the shrouds, theand; 'were as thick as thieves at a fair, whilst their elders were still ceremoniously manoeuvring on the outskirts of acquaintance. The sea, the ship, and the seamen were soon as familiar as home..'[53]

There was no serious illness on the *British Tar* and no loss of life. Two cases of opthalmia occurred as soon as the ship set sail; eye disease was endemic in the 19th century. One of these patients, after a relapse, required Brydone's skill as surgeon. He gave 'several successive free scarifications with the Lancet' before effecting a cure.[54]

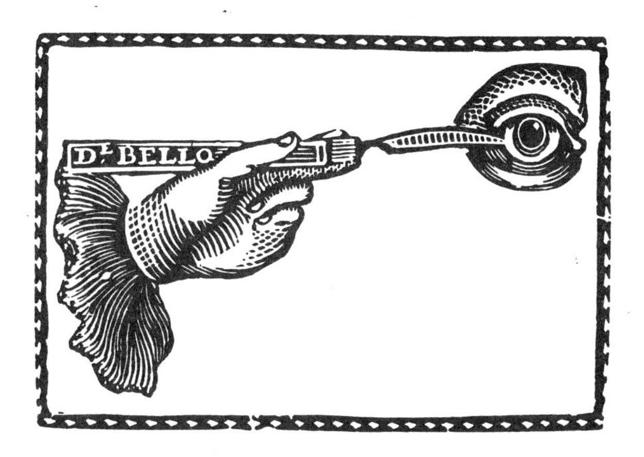

The worst health problem was an epidemic of measles affecting 12 of the children. There was a measles epidemic in Sussex and Hampshire during February and March of 1834. The Dittons' and the Colemans' youngest children, three of the Barton children, and the three Green children succumbed to the infection three days after the ship sailed; they obviously brought the infection with them. Later in the voyage, in the middle of May, four other cases were reported, one being little Francis West, the youngest of the West family, plus the youngest Perring child and the Snelling and Warren babies. All were regarded by Brydone as being 'favourable cases' in a 'minor epidemic'. Brydone probably regarded it as a minor epidemic in that none of the children died. Whether they were regarded as minor cases by their mothers is questionable, for it is not hard to imagine the discomfort and strain of nursing sick children within the restricted berth space. Mrs Ditton and Mary West were heavily pregnant. Mrs Ditton had at least one other child to care for and Mary West had six. By the time the second outbreak occurred, obviously incubated from the first, many people including Mrs Barton and Mrs Perring were suffering greatly from sea-sickness. The fathers probably helped out. Cobbett maintained that country labourers, especially those in Hampshire amongst whom he lived, were very loving and caring towards their little children, unlike middle class fathers who always expected their offspring to be cared for by servants. All the children recovered perfectly apart from the Bartons' eldest boy who, having had a severe attack of influenza before embarking, 'was in a very debilitated state'. This little boy was primarily the cause of the *British Tar* being detained later on at Grosse Island, the quarantine depot on the St Lawrence.

Brydone's immediate remedy for sea-sickness, which struck during the rough weather on the second half of the Atlantic passage, was a cup of coffee and a lie down. Hale had dosed his sufferers with brandy mixed with laudanum - a potent brew. Brydone made no note of issuing any laudanum. The women who suffered most from sea-sickness were Mrs Barton, Mrs and Miss Kemp, Mrs Gamblin, Mrs Martin and Mrs Perring. Only one married man sufferer was noted by Brydone, Mr Huntley. Several of the single men seem to have been victims, notably Henry Hammond, Abraham Muzzall, Henry Kemp, and three other men - Grafenstein, Pennicott and Tarrant. Mr Tarrant was unfortunate enough to follow the sea-sickness with a severe attack of constipation, a result, perhaps, of being dosed either by Brydone, or from his own personal medicine supply, with opium or laudanum, that 19th century remedy for numerous ills and upsets. Seeing his charges miserable with sickness and cold, Brydone had pea-soup made for them, which although it would not have quenched their thirst, would have supplied a warm, bland lining for their sore stomachs.

One other unfortunate incident, when the ship 'rolled much', was the upsetting of the cooking coppers before dinner. Thankfully there was no injury, except to the 'dirtied' beef, but the acting cook, John Barton, was frightened and had to be replaced at his post by Job Hodge.

One happy event was Mrs Ditton's confinement on 28 April and the birth of a daughter. The delivery took place within the cramped space of the family berth, in close proximity to the other family groups. Brydone was in attendance:

Imagine your humble servant cramped up for four hours in one of the Berths six feet square by two and a half feet high under the beams with Mrs D. and Mrs Green as attendant or Nurse. Contrast the want of comfort on board of a Ship with those usually found on shore on such occasions even in the humblest situation of life. Yet this woman did well requiring no other Medicine than a Dose of Castor oil for herself and her baby .[55]

It was fortunate for Mrs Ditton that this was not her first experience of childbirth, and she does indeed seem to have 'done well', as she and her husband enthusiastically joined the dancers on deck 17 days after her confinement.

A similar event on the *England* had occasioned a call by the married women for brandy to celebrate the birth. No such deputation came to Brydone following the arrival of the Ditton baby, neither did the sailors or married men make any appeal to him for their favourite grog, as they had done on the *England*. This may have shown a temperate spirit amongst the passengers and crew, or may re-affirm Brydone's role as a strict disciplinarian. He had, after all, been recruited on the premise that he would cut down on drunkenness. He was certainly much amused to be approached by Thomas Ditton on the Sunday following the birth and to be asked to christen the baby. Perhaps the Captain eventually did so, or perhaps the Dittons were forced to wait until they reached their new home. We were pleased to read that the little girl was amongst the party who finally made it to Blandford.

Medicines supplied to Revd.Thomas Sockett, Petworth Emigration Comittee, by Thomas Hodgkinson & Co., Snow Hill, London, 27th March, 1834 for use on the British Tar.

Item	Use
4oz citric acid	
2oz nitric acid (dilute)	
4oz sulphuric acid (dilute)	*for diarrhoea?*
4oz acacia powder	
8oz adepis lard	
2oz ammonium carbonate	*for cough mixtures*
1oz antimony tartrate	*for syphilis*
1oz anthimid	*camomile*
4oz tartaric acid	
10? silver (arg) nitrate	*cautery*
4oz camphor	*inhalant, liniment*
8oz calamine cream	*for itching*
1oz cetacei cream	
8oz cream of resin	*for wounds*
8oz cretae preparatae	*prepared chalk for wounds*
1oz copper sulphate	
1/2oz emp.cantharisemplastum	*plaster*
1/2oz emp.burgundie	
2oz ext.colocynth	*purgative*
2oz hydrate nitric oxide	*red mercuric oxide*
4oz hydrated submuriatis mercuric chloride	
6oz jalap	*purgative*
4oz ipecac.	*for cough or emetic*
4oz ipecac.comp.powder	
1 tin lin. saponis	*soap, liniment*
2oz liq.ammonia	*expectorant*
4oz liq.plumbi	*lead, for bruising*
6oz liq.val.c.c.	*valerian, stimulant*
8oz magnesium carbonate	*indigestion*
18lb magnesium sulphate	*epsom salts; for boils, purgative*
8oz ext.glycyrrhiza	*liquorice*
? oil menthol	*peppermint oil*
1 1/2? olive oil	
1/2? oil ricini	*castor oil*
4oz oil terebinth	*turpentine*
2oz opii colat	*dried extract of opium*
4oz pill.hydrarg	
1oz potassium nitrate	
8oz potassium bicarbonate	
2oz potassium supercarbonate	
1oz quinine	*fever, cramp*
6oz rhei powder	*rhubarb*
1/2oz scammonii resin	*purgative*
8oz senna	
8oz sodium carbonate	*soda*
4oz sodium tatrate	
4oz alkaline nitrate	*spirit ether nit.*
4oz alkaline sulphate	*spirit ether sulph.*
2oz lavand	*lavender*
8 oz ricilif rectified spirit	*pure alcohol*
1 1/2oz sulphur sublim.	
4oz tinct.catech.	*stimulant*
2oz tinct.benz.co.	*inhalation*
4oz tinct.cinch.	*for tonics*
4oz tinct.cinnamon	
4oz tinct.genti.	*bitter tonics*
4oz tinct.opii	*laudanum*
6oz tinct.rhei	*rhubarb*
8oz tinct.senna	
1oz unguentum hyd.forte	*strong mercury ointment*
1oz unguentum hyd.nitric mercuric nitr.	*ointment*
2oz zinc sulph.puri	*zinc sulphate, skin and eye lotions*
4oz zingiberis pdr.	*ginger powder, sea-sickness*

Instruments

Item	Use
2 bolas knives	
1 file	
6 bottles, 1/2 pint	
6 6oz octagons	
1/2 gross vial corks	
1 2oz measure	
1 mortar,metal	
1 mortar,wedgewood	
1 scales and weights	
1 sheepskin	*for bedsores*
1oz sponge	
1? lint	
1? fine tow	*for dressing wounds*
4yds adhesive plaster	
4yds flannel	
6yds calico	

Items used on voyage

- 5dr hydr.sub
- 4dr jalap
- 2dr pulv.scammonii
- 1oz liq.val.
- 2oz olive oil
- 4oz ricini oil
- 8lbs mag.sulph.
- 2oz tartaric acid
- 2oz sodium carbonate
- 4oz sulp.acid
- 1oz quinine sulp.

4: FOOD

Many of Brydone's Rules and Regulations were concerned with the supply and distribution of food. A Passenger Act of 1828 stipulated that emigrant ships must carry a daily ration, per person, of 1lb. of flour, bread, or biscuit, and a gallon of water, to prevent absolute starvation on the Atlantic crossing. Many emigrants had to bring all their own additional food. The P.E.C. preferred to provide daily rations for the emigrants on its ships.

Every person above 14 years counted as an adult, children under 14 had half rations. Infants under one year did not qualify for rations at all, presumably they were still being breast fed, or failing that had a little of the family's rations. No milk was provided but many babies in the 19th century, once they were weaned, had little or no milk.

The allowance for one adult, or two children , was as follows:

Sunday	*Beef 1lb. Potatoes 1 3/4lb.* *Rum and water 1/2 pint*
Monday	*Flour 1/2 lb. Butter 1/4 lb.* *Cheese 1/2 lb. Raisins 1/4 lb.*
Tuesday	*Pork 1lb. Potatoes 1 3/4 lb.* *Brandy and water 1/2 pint*
Wednesday	*Flour 1/2 lb. Butter 1/4 lb.* *Cheese 1/2 lb. Raisins 1/4 lb.*
Thursday	*Beef 1lb. Potatoes 1 3/4 lb.* *Rum and water 1/2 pint*
Friday	*Flour 1/2 lb. Butter 1/4 lb.* *Cheese 1/2 lb. Raisins 1/4 lb.*
Saturday	*Pork 1lb. Potatoes 1 3/4 lb.* *Brandy and water 1/2 pint*

Every morning between 6 and 7 a.m. Bread 1/2 lb. Water 1/2 gallon. Every Saturday Tea 2 ozs, Sugar 1/4 lb.(56)

In 1988 the Southern Water Authority reckoned that a ton of water, 220 gallons, was sufficient for a family of four for two days. The same family on the *British Tar* would have had 8 gallons for two days. A ton of water had to last four adults for nine weeks. The 'sweetness' of the water was questionable, for Brydone admitted that 'water on board of a Ship is at no time (without a filter) a very palatable beverage.'(57)

The tea ration of 2 ozs. per person per week could make six mugs of tea per day. This could take roughly three pints of water from the daily allowance leaving five pints per adult for drinking, cooking, soaking the salt meat and diluting the rum or brandy allowance. There is no reference to the proportion of spirits to water in Brydone's schedule but on the *England* brandy had been given in not less than three times its quantity of water.

The food seems reasonable in quantity and variety assuming it was edible when it was dished out, which was not always so. The apparently generous meat ration would include bone - witness the bone lodged in the w.c. The P.E.C. admitted that on their earlier ships the passengers had been unable to eat the highly salted Irish beef provided, preferring to subsist on bread or biscuit. So many emigrants complained in their letters home that on the *"England"* and the *British Tar* the P.E.C. provided bacon and pork from Petworth, and beef which was salted at Portsmouth the week before departure. Cobbett would have agreed with the emigrants' complaints for he described as villainous the taste of 'barrel pork' and 'sea-jonk' - the salt meat supplied to ships and so called from its toughness and likeness to old rope ends. Cobbett maintained that very fat mutton and beef were best for salting, not lean meat which was good for nothing. 'Poor fellows on board of ships are compelled to eat it , but it is a very bad thing.'(58) The potato ration of 1 3/4 lbs. per adult also seems generous but in April, when the ship sailed, potatoes would have already been stored all winter and there must have been considerable wastage.

If the meat and other foods were palatable then the diet provided, although spartan to some, must have seemed quite satisfactory to others, and a feast to those who, like the Wests, had been living largely on gallons of flour or bread doled out by the poor law authorities. Brydone wrote that 'several of the young men expressed a wish that the voyage might last for six months'(59) and one hopes that the West children looked better when they arrived than when they embarked. Butcher's meat, beef and mutton, was largely unknown in the average labourer's diet, although some home cured pork and bacon was common in Sussex. Cobbett said he saw a pig at almost every labourer's cottage when he rode through the county in 1830. Nevertheless, the staple diet of the farm worker and his family throughout the week was bread and cheese, the bread often of poor quality and the cheese in short supply. If the labourer was lucky enough to have a garden or allotment he could grow vegetables, although these were often regarded as very much second class food and eaten somewhat reluctantly.

Sockett and the managers of Petworth Poorhouse provided a similar diet for the Poorhouse inmates in 1833 to that of the *British Tar* passengers. On the whole, the Poorhouse diet was more generous, with meat or gruel for dinner plus bread and cheese for supper every day whereas the *British Tar* traveller had either meat or cheese per day and no gruel, but their meat or cheese ration was considerably larger. The Poorhouse inhabitant also had fresh vegetables. None was provided on board ship. Again, April is a bad time for vegetables and fruit. Presumably the emigrants did not get scurvy en-route to Canada because there was not time for it to develop. The Petworth Poorhouse diet also provided beer whereas the *British Tar* passengers got none. They, however, only had to stick it out for a few weeks and they then hoped to be living well in their new life. For the inhabitants of the Poorhouse the long term outlook was far from rosy, with the implementation of new poor law regulations from 1834 onwards their diet was to be severely pruned of anything regarded as faintly luxurious, such as meat pudding, much to Sockett's anger.

On board ship the emigrants were divided into messes. Brydone says in his log that there were twenty messes, although in an earlier letter he said there were only eight men appointed as heads of the messes,(see his Rules and Regulations). Whatever the number, each mess drew its rations at ten o'clock in the morning and John Gamblin, William Green and William Martin took it in turns to see there was no undue delay and everyone got their fair share. Each mess may have put their rations of meat and potatoes together, cooked them en-masse in a communal pot, and doled them out in what seemed fair shares. On the other hand, each family may have cooked its own rations sepa-

Scale of Victualling the Emigrants to Canada per British Tar in 1834

Sunday	Beef 1 lb Potatoes 1 3/4 lb Rum & Water 1/2 Pint
Monday	Flour 1/2 lb Cheese 1/2 lb Butter 1/4 lb Raisins 1/4 lb
Tuesday	Pork 1 lb Potatoes 1 3/4 lb Brandy & Water 1/2 Pint
Wednesday	Flour 1/2 lb Cheese 1/2 lb Butter 1/4 lb Raisins 1/4 lb
Thursday	Beef 1 lb Potatoes 1 3/4 lb Rum & Water 1/2 Pint
Friday	Flour 1/2 lb Cheese 1/2 lb Butter 1/4 lb Raisins 1/4 lb
Saturday	Pork 1 lb Potatoes 1 3/4 lb Brandy & Water 1/2 Pint
Morning Daily at Six & Ten	Bread 1/2 lb ~~Potatoes~~ 1/4 lb Water 1/2 Gallon
Every Saturday	Tea 2 oz Sugar 1/4 lb

Br.

W. M. Brydone
Superintendent

Polworth June 6th 1833.

At a Special Vestry held this Day ~~according to~~ notice given in Church June 2nd in Order to make out a Bill of Fare for the Poorhouse ——

Present the Rev. J. W. Sockett
Mr. James Ireland
Edward Jo. Sta[illegible]
John Wright
John Brown
Thomas Sherwin
James Green
William Bicknell
Edward Butt

The following Bill of Fare was agreed upon accordingly

~~Monday~~
Sunday { Breakfast. Gruel, as much as they please.
Dinner. Meat puddings 10 oz. or Boiled Pork or Bacon 6 oz. } Bread 4 oz. Vegetables, what they please
Supper. Bread 7 oz. Cheese 2 oz. or Butter 1 oz.

Monday { Breakfast. as before —
Dinner. Soup 3 lb 2 oz.
Supper. Same as Sunday.

Tuesday { Breakfast. as before
Dinner. ~~Bacon or Pork~~, Same as Sunday.
Supper. as before

Wednesday { Breakfast as before
Dinner. Suet Pudding 1 lb. Vegetables.
Supper. as before

Thursday { ~~B~~ Same as Sunday throughout

Friday { Breakfast. as before
Dinner. Soup. 3 lb 2 oz.
Supper. as before

Saturday { Breakfast. as before
Dinner. Bread 9 oz. Cheese 2 oz.
Supper. Bread 8 oz. Cheese 2 oz.

if Cake be given at any time for Supper ~~at any time~~ instead of Bread and Cheese the quantity to be 10 oz.

Beer. During Dinner and Supper what they please

~~Men who go out to~~

rately, putting their meat and potatoes to boil in marked nets or other containers in the communal boiler. As the *British Tar* had only two cooking hearths for 135 people it is difficult to imagine how anyone got near enough to cook anything even in communal pots. Cooking and water heating must have gone on all day.

The Poorhouse people had meat pudding under Sockett's administration for he said that Sussex people were very fond of pudding. Suet is not listed in the *British Tar* rations but the emigrants could have taken it with them or substituted part of their butter ration as fat. With their rations the Voice family could thus have made boiled meat or bacon pudding; 'swimmers'-plain boiled suet pudding served with butter or sugar; Sussex pond pudding; and 'hard dumplings'- made only from flour, water and salt - which only a Sussex woman could make successfully, comments Tony Wales in *A Sussex Garland.* [60]

If Elizabeth, or any of the other women, had taken the Dutch oven suggested by Hale, they could bake Lardy

Johns - a kind of scone made from flour, fat, sugar and raisins; or Coager Cake - a pastry round filled with sugar and a few raisins; or plum heavies - a similar mixture with the raisins rolled into the pastry. In *A Dictionary of the Sussex Dialect,* published in 1875, The Rev. W.D. Parish said that the inhabitants of Hellingly were well known for making coager cakes, and plum heavies were a unique Sussex delicacy joyfully recognised as such by Sussex colonials. A Dutch oven or a trivet would also enable the passengers to grill a slice of bacon, or toast their cheese.

Any fancy cooking that the emigrants did must have been largely in the first weeks of their voyage for after 26 April there was bad weather and when the sea was rough it was almost impossible to cook, the cooking boilers overturned, and sea sickness broke out. An emigrant on a contemporary ship gave a graphic picture of the poor traveller recovering a little from sickness :

then when the gale subsides, sickness abates, hunger succeeds, and the almost famished wretch, unwashed and unshaven, holds on with one hand, while in the other is held the frying pan with his morsel of salt pork, [with] which he must wait, perhaps in the rain, or when the sea is breaking over, till his turn at the fire place comes [61]

It was at this point, off the Newfoundland Banks, that Brydone organised pea-soup for the people suffering so badly from cold, thirst and sea-sickness. He bought four gallons of dried peas from Captain Crawford and produced a pint of soup for everyone; trusting that the P.E.C.would excuse the expense.

The more fortunate emigrants would, as we have suggested, have taken extra food with them. Pickled onions and other pickles would add interest to the meat and cheese, jam and preserves would sweeten the bread for the children, and dried herbs could flavour the boiled meat. John Luck, a later emigrant to America, and an experienced traveller prudently took some bicarbonate of soda to raise the flour for little rolls. Hale recommended barley for broth; oatmeal - very wholesome and useful in sickness; a keg of pickled tripe as a more palatable alternative to ship's salt beef; and cubes of portable soup. The 18th century cookery writer, Hannah Glasse, in her book *The Art of Cookery Made Plain and Easy* gave recipes for pea soup and portable soup. The latter was a rich stock reduced and reduced, dried into little glue-like cakes and stored between sheets of paper. It was reconstituted with boiling water, much like a modern stockcube. She devoted a whole chapter to recipes for ' Captains of Ships' including one for Catchup to keep twenty Years' using strong stale beer, anchovies, shallots, mushrooms and spices; 'when bottled you may carry it to the Indies'. She also gave instructions for preserving tripe.[62]

It is noticeable that many emigrants' letters sent home from Canada dwell at length, and with pleasure, on the cheapness and variety of their food. Cornelius Voice gives details of the meat, the fowls, the vegetables, the sugar and treacle, that the family are now producing and eating. His account of his daughter, Elizabeth's, marriage comes only as a hasty footnote.

PART 5: THE CREW

What of the man who was accustomed to be closely stowed on board ship and to eat highly salted Irish beef? - the British tar.

On that Thursday afternoon in April as the *British Tar* slipped down channel under a 'soldiers wind', the crew would be busily engaged securing for sea, adjusting sails and tidying decks. Their foul weather gear dangling from pegs in the fo'c'sle would rustle and swing from side to side as the vessel came out from under the lee of the Isle of Wight, and the channel chop began. If any had just signed on they might be feeling satisfied that they had got a berth in a well found ship.

Built at Sunderland in 1824 the ship was ten years old and rated as A.1 at Lloyds of London, her port of registry. This meant that she had been built to specifications in respect of strength, safety, and cargo carrying capacity laid down by this world famous maritime association of underwriters, and therefore listed in *Lloyd's Register of Shipping*; the entry confirming her tonnage as 383, her owner named as Forrest, her master Captain Crawford. She was advertised as being copper bottomed and fastened. This related to the sheathing of the wooden hull, below the water line, with sheets of copper secured with copper bolts, to protect her timbers from the ravages of the teredo worm to which oak was very subject. Copper bottoming also prevented the formation of barnacles on the hull which otherwise would accumulate inches thick and impede the speed of the ship through the water. The words 'copper-bottomed' have come to be accepted as a term for security and trustworthiness - a certainty!

The ship was a brig, a two masted vessel, square-rigged on both fore and main masts, with fore-and-aft staysails, jibs, and a spanker. She would have been about 150 feet long on the waterline. Brigs were widely used in days of sail for short-sea coastal trading voyages, for example the nineteenth-century colliers from the Tyne.

She is quoted on the sailing posters as 383 Tons registered Burthen. This would appear to be incorrect phraseology; perhaps coined in ignorance by the printer. Burthen was an eighteenth-century term used to express a ship's tonnage, or carrying capacity. It was based on the number of tuns of wine she could carry in her holds and was probably well outdated by 1834. The registered tonnage was more likely to have been what was known as Builders Old Measurement, (B.O.M.) which was calculated from a mathematical formula concerning the ratio of the length of the ship to the beam, divided by a constant. This method of measurement had been laid down by Act of Parliament in 1773, and remained in force until the advent of steam powered ships constructed of iron.

With nearly 150 souls onboard, only a very small handful - the few members of the crew - would know what to expect or what was expected of them. Passengers would have to quickly learn the basic rules of life at sea - the utilisation of space, conservation of water, cooking arrangements, the inadvisability of throwing anything to windward, and the provision of the 'necessary'!

The crew would probably be only too happy to show the passengers around, especially the children; it would be novel having them on board and vastly different from their usual cargo. The sailors would explain the inherent dangers of life afloat, emphasising the danger of fire. Smoking was, in Brydone's rules, forbidden anywhere between decks - other than in the immediate vicinity of the galley in the break of the fo'c'sle.

The deck area here would be covered with a brick lining, and there would be rows of sand filled fire buckets for ash trays. Here the two extra stoves for the use of the passengers were set up alongside the ship's normal galley stove; warm and sheltered from the elements this would no doubt have been a popular gathering place.

Life in the crew's quarters would be no improvement upon that of the passengers. They lived, ate their meals, and slept, crammed into the constantly pitching fo'c'sle, slinging their hammocks close packed in their allotted space of between 14 and 18 inches. If they could arrange it so that men on opposite watches slung alternately, every other hammock in a row would be vacant at night and they might not bang into each other with the roll of the ship. Working a watch and watch system, (four hours on and four hours off) - the time off constantly being interrupted by being called on deck to assist in tacking, wearing or shortening sail, - was physically exhausting. The most sleep a man could get at night was a broken seven hours in two sessions, but only four the following night, - assuming he wasn't called out for extra sail duties, - and so on, in rotation. The sailor's bedding, a 'donkey's breakfast' was a straw mattress, and two thick blankets. His outer clothing rolled up would serve for a pillow, and a short length of timber would be used as a stretcher to spread his nettles wider at the head of the hammock. Sheets would be unknown. A man would often keep a change of clothing in his hammock, something dry to change into when he came below if he got drenched during a night watch. Their mess would have the tarry, musty smell of old rope, be noisy, dark, lit only by tallow dips, ('purser's glims'), and constantly damp. In foul weather a certain amount of water would always leak through the deckhead, as the upper deck seams worked, and drip from the deckhead onto bedding, accumulate, and slop about as the ship rolled. Constantly on the move even in calm weather the mess was never on an even keel either, as the ship heeled to the wind.

The emigrants might well have woken from their fitful first night's sleep, before first light, to the sounds of the upper deck being washed down. After a spell in port the ship's weather decks would be dirty from the constant foot traffic loading stores. The morning watchmen, turned out at four o'clock, barefooted, with their bell-bottomed trousers rolled up to their knees, wielding scrubbers and clanking buckets, and would rig pumps to wet the decks down with sea water. After sprinkling sand on the wet deck, heavy holystones would be hauled up and down over it, smaller 'prayer books' would be used around fittings and in corners by sailors on their hands and knees. After rinsing off, sand and muck would disappear into the scuppers and over the side, surplus water being swabbed and the deck left to dry; whilst all ropes ends were coiled or cheesed down neatly, and the brightwork cleaned, the cleaning gear could then be returned to the washdeck locker. On the morrow during this daily ritual at sea, the newly selected cooks of the emigrants' messes would be picking their way for'rd to draw their daily bread and fresh water ration. By now it would be about seven o'clock and there would be other signs of life on board. No doubt some of the passengers would have found their way up top for some fresh air and to see where they were. Children would be exploring and parties of people tooing and frowing between the hatches and the galley. The ship's cook would have flashed up his fires shortly after five, and by now have something boiling away in his coppers. The watch below would have been called, hammocks lashed up and stowed, tables rigged in the fo'c'sle, and all hands except the helmsman, lookout, and mate on duty would have slipped below for breakfast. The first full day at sea was well under way.

After breakfast the watch below would busy themselves clearing away the meal. The mess table would be scrubbed down and stowed away, the deck swept and perhaps swabbed down, ports opened and the mess aired. It was important to keep the ship clean, dry, and well ventilated, and the mate would doubtless be doing rounds later. The watch on deck and any spare hands would also be kept busy employed in ship husbandry duties. There was always cordage which required renewing, chafed ropework to be repaired or sails to be patched and stitched. The carpenter and boatswain would soon find employment for idle hands, especially if after sounding the bilges it was found necessary to operate the bilge pump! The cook of the mess and the Captain's cabin boy, (joined for this trip by Mr. Upton, chosen by Brydone to be his steward), would pass the forenoon in preparing the midday meal together with the ship's cook, and in cleaning up the mess and galley utensils.

Having taken a reliable departure fix before losing sight of land, daily, as noon approached, the master and one of the mates would appear on deck with their sextants. Noon was reported when the sun reached the meridian and the clock put forward or back accordingly. A seaman aft would haul in the log which trailed astern to record the ship's speed and distance run during the watch. Eight bells would be rung and the order 'hands to dinner' passed as the watch changed. The men who had scrubbed the decks that morning would take the watch again, whilst those who had had the middle watch and been on deck between midnight and four a.m., and again from eight until noon, could now retire below, eat, clear away the meal and 'get their heads down'.Supper would be eaten soon after four p.m.. Before sunset during the dog watches, lifebuoys would be placed in position, pumps rigged, bilges checked, lamps trimmed, hammocks retrieved from the nettings and slung, and the ship prepared for another night at sea.

The First watchmen would relieve at eight p.m. and a

mate would do rounds to check that all was shipshape for the night. Lamps would be extinguished or shielded, and helmsmen and lookouts would look forward to their reliefs coming up at midnight. A few minutes before they were due on watch the middle watchmen would tumble out hoping the cook had left them a brew on a dampened down stove. A favour like this might be returned by them flashing up his stove for him before they went off watch at four a.m. The first watchmen would no doubt troop for'rd hoping not to be called out during their brief time off for a sail change, and peace would settle on the ship again, only occasional quiet helm orders or reports breaking the silence. Silence that is from the seaman's point of view, but the sound of the sea slapping against the side, the wind in the rigging, the creaking and groaning of timbers and tiller ropes, or the sliding across deck of a piece of unsecured luggage might cause many an emigrant to pass a fitful night. All too soon it would be eight bells, the watches would change and washdeck lockers be thrown open for buckets and scrubbers as dawn broke astern, and another day began.The fair easterly wind blew the *British Tar* down channel past Lands End and she was on her way into the Atlantic as Sunday came and went; a day on which the ship's routine would be relaxed - the nearest thing to a 'day off' at sea - and attendance at Brydone's prayer meeting after an extra specially good scrub down and whitening of the upper deck might have been a welcome change. No doubt the crew would have turned out in their smartest gear and eyed the women in their finery.

On Saturday 26 April, almost halfway across, the weather began to break. At first the rain would have been welcome. Sails would have been rigged to collect as much water as possible for washing clothing. As the weather got up and spindrift began to come over the bulwarks, hands would begin securing any gear that might come adrift; the heavy sea making the vessel roll and ship water in the scuppers which would soon find its way over hatch coamings and down below. The wind shifted round during the night, increasing to a strong north westerly gale which would have had the watch below tumbling out to get soaked to the skin assisting in taking in sail.

By the morning watch the wind had veered to the north and dropped as quickly as it had got up. Indeed, Brydone was able to hold a Sunday morning prayer meeting a few hours later. The noon position was logged as being Latitude 46 degrees 3 minutes North, Longitude 37 minutes 8 degrees West, well past mid Atlantic. They were now heading for the shallower waters of the Newfoundland Bank, well known for its fishing grounds, fogs and icebergs - which they could expect to sight in another seven to ten days.

The weather stayed fair just long enough to see the completion of Mrs Ditton's confinement. The birth of a baby on board would have been seen as a good omen by the crew - very good 'joss' for the ship. Tales of baptisms in a ship's bell may have prompted Mr Ditton's intrepid advance to Brydone, who up till then had perhaps seemed to him to be his spiritual advisor, (with his Sunday prayers and sermon), as well as his wife's medical guardian. Although this advance was surprising to Brydone [63] it may have seemed natural to the crew in their ignorance; after all, they may have remembered the adage that a Captain can perform marriage ceremonies at sea in place of a minister. With his advanced years and naval bearing the Superintendent might have seemed to be far above their Captain in the pecking order, and thus probably capable of doing anything.

On the other hand, and more likely, the crew may well have put Ditton up to it as a practical joke!

On Tuesday 29 April,the wind veered again and blew a strong gale from the west. It is possible they rode out the gale to a sea anchor, but anyway Brydone praised the shiphandling of Captain Crawford, and the seaworthiness of the ship herself.[64] The gale lasted three days, and tempestuous weather continued for another seven days, during which adverse winds alternated with favourable ones. It was getting much colder too, and wet seamen might huddle around the galley stoves when they were relieved, trying to get some circulation going in their hands and feet. Extra lookouts would be posted to keep watch for icebergs. Living conditions in the fo'c'sle would be unbearable. The crashing and shuddering as the bows lifted and plunged into the seas,'hitting the milestones',then the corkscrew motion as the ship fought off the immense weight of water and rose to the next wave, would constantly throw the men off balance, sending their gear tumbling out of lockers or breaking adrift from bulkheads.

Suddenly on Thursday 8 May, dawn broke to a glassy smooth sea, the wind having moved round to S.S.W. was blowing bitterly cold over their port quarter. Icebergs were sighted three times during the day and the ship's noon position put her on the Newfoundland Bank. Grand Banks fishing vessels were sighted the following day and the leadsman found bottom at 50 fathoms using soundings to help confirm their westing. Captain Crawford would be anxious to know his exact longitude, as soon he would need to alter course northwards to make for the Cabot Strait, the entrance to the Gulf of St. Lawrence. During the dog watches on Saturday evening they were fortunate enough to fall in with the *Caledonian*, four weeks out from Hull and bound for Miramichi in New Brunswick. The two masters compared notes. The master of the *Caledonian* had worked out his position by chronometer; that is he had found his longitude by comparing the local time and the corresponding Greenwich Mean Time. The difference in time would be converted to degrees longitude. By this method his position differed from Captain Crawford's dead reckoning position the previous day by more than one degree. Sunday 11 May dawned cold and wet, the temperature a degree below freezing, with the wind in the same quarter. By the end of the morning watch visibility had closed in and they were in a Grand Banks' fog. The bell on the fo'c'sle would have been rung in short bursts to announce their presence, alternating with the lookouts straining their ears to hear the fog signals of any other vessel in the vicinity.Their exact position would still have concerned the master, striving to make a landfall. On Monday soundings revealed they were now in forty fathoms, and Tuesday brought rain to clear the fog.

Wednesday 14 May, started calm but foggy. By noon a fresh breeze blew the fog away, and at three o'clock in the afternoon the snow covered peaks of the Long Range mountains of Newfoundland came into sight. The Captain being keen to make his landfall ran in on a bearing until about ten miles off shore when he tacked, having recognised Cape Ray from his chart and pilot. Dead reckoning navigation was now over; he could fix his position with certainty, the *British Tar* was twenty miles south by east of Cape Ray, the south west corner of Newfoundland which guarded the Cabot Strait.

As if to celebrate, the following days were remarkably fine, giving the crew a chance to air their bedding and ventilate their quarters. Bird Island was passed - the ship was in the Gulf of St .Lawrence - but during the first watch on Friday the weather deteriorated again; fresh breezes brought hail and rain, the rain getting heavier during the night, but at noon on Saturday a fix was taken on Cape Gaspe, twenty five miles distant on the port bow. A course was directed to pass between Cape Gaspe and Anticosti Island, the light of which was raised ten miles distant on Sunday. This island guards the mouth of the St.Lawrence River. At eight bells in the morning watch Captain Crawford picked up a pilot, Mr Peltie, off the mouth of the river Magdalen opposite the Seven Islands, for the passage up the St.Lawrence to Grosse Island.

CANADA

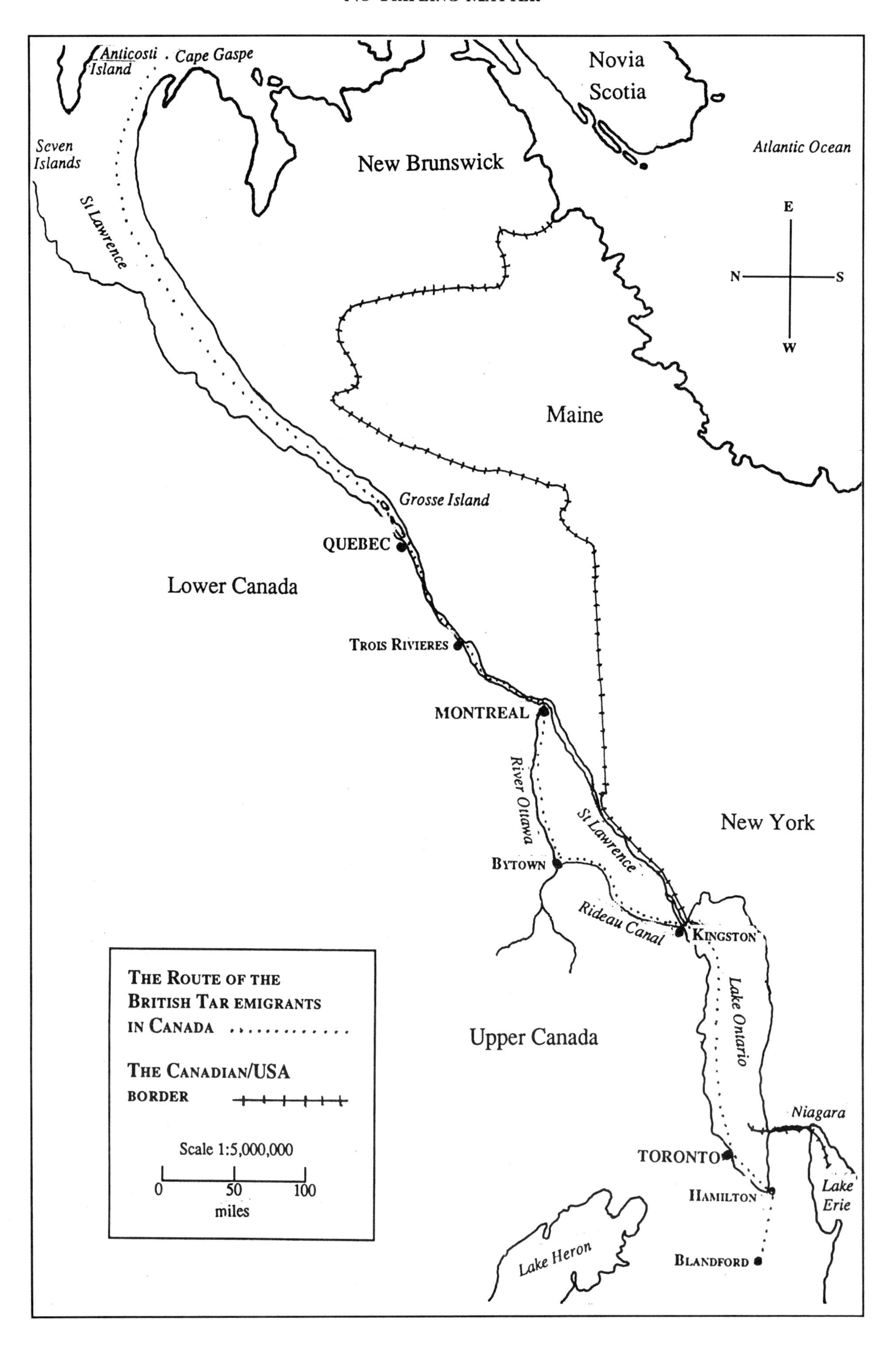
Anticosti Island
Cape Gaspe
Novia Scotia
Seven Islands
New Brunswick
Atlantic Ocean
St Lawrence
E
N
S
W
Maine
Grosse Island
QUEBEC
Lower Canada
TROIS RIVIERES
MONTREAL
River Ottawa
St Lawrence
New York
BYTOWN
Rideau Canal
KINGSTON
Lake Ontario
THE ROUTE OF THE BRITISH TAR EMIGRANTS IN CANADA
THE CANADIAN/USA BORDER
Scale 1:5,000,000
0
50
100
miles
Upper Canada
Niagara
TORONTO
HAMILTON
Lake Erie
Lake Heron
BLANDFORD

1: TO MONTREAL.

We have entered the River St.Lawrence by storm - the brunt of the Battle is over. Not a single loss has been sustained on the voyage. I can now respond with a ***Hurrah;*** wrote Brydone to Sockett.[65]

On 23 May, after a voyage of 35 days the *British Tar* arrived at Grosse Island and anchored off-shore along with the 30 or so other ships awaiting clearance. The passengers were no doubt delighted to have what could be expected as the worst part of the journey behind them. Although they still had some 200 miles to go on the St.Lawrence before they would leave the *British Tar* at Montreal and face the journey on rivers, canals, lakes and overland, before arriving at their new homes. It was to be a further 30 days before they arrived at their final destination of Blandford.

Grosse Island, a small island about 30 miles from Quebec, was taken over in 1832 as a quarantine depot for emigrants arriving in Canada. At that time there was an epidemic of cholera in Scotland in areas from which many of the emigrants, including the Irish, sailed for Canada. The poor and crowded conditions on board some of the emigrant ships only added to the problem by spreading the plague on the ships and bringing even more cholera into Canada.[66]

In an effort to stem this epidemic, and others, a Proclamation of the Executive Council of Lower Canada dated 27 March 1834 (of which possibly Brydone was not aware before sailing) made it a requirement that all ships with cases of cholera, fever, small pox or severe cases of scarlatina or measles on board shall be put in quarantine, and all patients suffering from any of these diseases shall be sent to hospital. This information was passed to the *British Tar* by the Harbour Master who went along-side shortly after she had anchored. Dr. Fortie, the Inspecting Physician, then went aboard, mustered the passengers, directed that the yellow 'quarantine' flag be hoisted, and the four recent case of measles along with the convalescents be sent to the hospital ashore. Mr and Mrs Barton's boy, who was convalescent but debilitated from having had influenza prior to the measles, was sent ashore, to benefit from the better nursing, medical attention and hospital diet said to be available there.

Brydone was annoyed at this turn of events. Half the townships in Lower Canada were in the grip of a cholera epidemic and he could see no good reason for removing his charges from a clean ship, where the general health was good, to the hospital on the island where disease was rampant. The regulations also required that every person who had chaff or straw in his bed was to throw it overboard and was not allowed to replace it. This also annoyed Brydone. His people were going to Montreal, some ten days sailing, not like other emigrants who would reach Quebec in 24 hours. This was even more annoying, doubtless, to some of the pregnant women on board who would be deprived of the comfort of their mattresses.

Two days later orders were received to land the passengers and their baggage for inspection, in spite of them having washed their clothes and bedding aboard the ship whilst it was lying off the island. They were taken ashore by small boats; a dangerous procedure, for a number of people in other ships had been drowned getting in and out of these ferry boats.

We can try to imagine the scene as the passengers crowded on the ship's deck with their baggage. The Voices with their large family, Mrs Ditton with her little baby, the Wests with their seven children and Mary West pregnant, all trying perhaps to help each other and keep their own family or group together, and all the time the hustle and bustle as the sailors tried to get as many people and their baggage as possible in each boat. Having all safely landed on the island the wind came up, and as the tide was unfavourable they had to spend the night ashore. The ship's crew had also been ashore, got drunk, become unruly, and been put in the guard house, so that Brydone and Captain Crawford were unable to return to the ship. However, they were more fortunate than the passengers in that they were invited to dine ashore with Captain Reid, the Port Commandant, who later took them back to their ship in his own boat.

The next day Brydone took bread and cheese to the people ashore. The ship was fumigated and by the evening all passengers and their baggage were safely re-embarked, although William Dighton had managed to fall in the water, fortunately without harm.

On the 31 May, eight days after anchoring at Grosse Island, the ship was released from quarantine, the little Barton boy was brought on board from hospital, and at noon they were on their way - only to find a contrary wind and they had to anchor for the night.

No doubt Brydone was pleased to get all his people off Grosse Island without any loss of life. He was however still smarting at the treatment they had had to suffer and annoyed that after bringing his people so far in safety and good spirits, they were now upset and distressed at being detained for nine days, at having to go ashore with all their baggage , and remain there all night without shelter other than an open shed which had been barely sufficient room for the women and children:

I do not blame the authorities of Grosse Isle, for any of these occurrences; I am satisfied, that the accommodation, and assistance, at the place, is not adequate, to the duties of the station; and I believe, they have little, or no discretionary power. The principal place, where persons in quarantine, at Grosse Isle, are sent to wash, and clean their clothes, and themselves, is a continued succession, of small, rugged, projecting points, of rock, where the filth accumulates, in the hollows, and eddies, until the winds scatter it abroad, over the clean, and unclean;...(67)

Brydone saw no reason why the inspection of the immigrants and their baggage could not be carried out on board, saving trouble and annoyance and avoiding 'the risk of property and life'.

By 5 May 1834, 327 ships had arrived at Grosse Island, bringing 654 cabin passengers and 10,919 steerage passengers, 11,564 emigrants in all. As all steerage passengers had to go ashore for inspection it is no wonder that the place was dirty and littered with rubbish. An emigrant who had arrived two years earlier gave a graphic description of Grosse Island. Susanna Moodie, in her biography *Roughing it in the Bush*, tells how on anchoring at Grosse Island in August 1832 she saw the surrounding scenery with a thrill of wonder and delight:

The rocky isle in front, with its neat farm-houses at the eastern point, and its high bluff at the western extremity, crowned with the telegraph - the middle space occupied by tents and sheds for the cholera patients, and its wooded shores dotted over with motley groups - added greatly to the picturesque effect of the land scene. Then the broad, glittering river, covered with boats darting to and fro, conveying passengers from twenty-five vessels, of various size and tonnage, which rode at anchor.

However as a cabin passenger she was not included in those who had to go ashore - her servant took her bedding and clothes to be washed - nevertheless she had a desire to go ashore herself and was therefore delighted when the Officer in Command of the Island invited her husband and herself to spend the afternoon with him on a tour of the island. She went on to say:

A crowd of many hundred Irish emigrants had been landed during the present and former day and all this motley crew - men, women, and children, who were not confined by sickness to the sheds (which greatly resembled cattle-pens) - were employed in washing clothes or spreading them out on the rocks and bushes to dry.

The men and boys were in the water, while the women, with their scanty garments tucked above their knees, were tramping their bedding in tubs or in holes in the rocks, which the retiring tide had left half full of water. Those who did not possess washing tubs, pails, or iron pots, or could not obtain access to a hole in the rocks, were running to and fro, screaming and scolding in no measured terms. The confusion of Babel was among them... We were literally stunned by the strife of tongues, I shrank, with feelings almost akin to fear, from the hard-featured, sunburnt women as they elbowed rudely past me.(68)

It seems that things were little different when the *British Tar* arrived two years later. Brydone says that his people were cast down and annoyed at their treatment at Grosse Island. Their feelings must have been similar to those of Susanna Moodie in that after being at sea for seven weeks and gaining a favourable impression of their new country as they sailed up the St.Lawrence, they first set foot on land in such a dreadful place, and had to contend with the people they found there. They must have looked forward with some trepidation and apprehension as to what they would find on the remainder of their journey and at their final destination.

After anchoring for the night of 31 May, just off Grosse Island, the next day brought a light breeze and on a remarkably fine day they continued their voyage, passing the beautiful Isle of Orleans. This scenery and outlook did much to lift the spirits of the passengers:

The people highly delighted, those who formerly hesitated from the sterile, and [monotonous] appearance of the land giving an opinion, now yeilding [sic] their ready approbation 'This will do'. (69)

Later on the same day they anchored at Quebec. Here they were delayed for some time for the obligatory inspection by the Harbour Master, Custom House and Quarantine Officers, and by a change of pilot who refused to sail until the following morning.

William Warren, his wife and child left the ship here, but it is not recorded if this was a prearranged departure.

Next morning, on 2 June, they set sail again, but a storm blew up and they were obliged to shelter in Wolf's Cove. As the weather did not improve, Captain Crawford and Brydone went ashore and hired a steam boat, the *St.George*, to tow the *British Tar* up river to Montreal. About midnight the boat arrived, took the ship in tow and they were on their way again.

They passed through the rapids of Richlieu during the night, and in the morning arrived at Trois Riviere, about half way to Montreal, where they took on a supply of wood for fuel. Leaving Trois Riviere they passed through the narrow channel leading into Lake St.Peter, and after an easy passage over the Lake had to pass through the rapids at Sorel. They waited some two hours for the tide to bring enough water for them to navigate the rocky shallows and narrows.

In the early morning of 4 June they arrived at Montreal, which then, as now, was an important and busy port having an extensive harbour, a large population, fine houses in wide and regular streets, and 'shops as large as any in Lewes', as Henry Harwood noted. (70)

Here Brydone was able to officially complain about the treatment they had received at Grosse Island. He also pointed out that during their enforced stay at the island the wind had been favourable for them to sail up the river, but as soon as they were allowed to sail the wind changed and they had had to hire a steam boat to tow them to Montreal. This tow cost £53 7s 10d, plus a passenger charge of £21 7s 6d; plus the daily cost at Grosse Island of £6 15s 0d - a total of £135 15s 4d. He was so incensed that after the whole voyage was over, and before leaving Canada, he wrote to the Emigration Officer in Quebec to claim this expense - to no avail.

Brydone then made contact with the Hon. Peter McGill, the Chairman of the Montreal Emigration and Sanitary Committee, who gave assistance and information about the routes ahead, both by the older St.Lawrence route, or the new one by the Rideau Canal. Brydone decided to use the northern route through the Rideau Canal, the first time this would be used by a P.E.C. party. This route would enable the party to be kept together, for larger boats were available, and they would only have to change boats once between Montreal and Toronto. As there was little habitation along the way, liquors and spirits would be difficult to obtain and it would be easier for Brydone to maintain order; many emigrants and ships' crews celebrated their safe arrival in Canada by orgies of drunkeness.

Mr Cushing, the local Agent of the newly established British Land Company, arranged for a boat to carry the party from Montreal to Kingston via the Rideau Canal, at a cost of 12s 6d per person, including 1cwt of baggage each. The boat was considerably better than the open Durham boats used on former occasions and the cause of many complaints. This boat was fully decked with a large cabin containing fixed bed places for most of the women, girls and children. The remainder of the females and the married and single men were to be accommodated below decks, the positions so arranged that the married men were placed between the single men and the females - Brydone again ever mindful of the morals of his charges.

The following day was spent in off-loading the *British Tar* and loading the boat for Kingston. All the baggage, and provisions enough for eight days, were transported in Mr. Cushing's carts at no charge, to his store-house, and after weighing and assessing excess charges on the 56cwt extra, all was loaded on the boat. A supply of straw was obtained to refill the bed ticks which had been emptied at Grosse Island. The medicine chest was sealed and handed over to Capt. Crawford for conveyance to England; after Brydone had prudently removed an ounce of Quinine and two ounces of diluted sulphuric acid in case of 'the occurrence of Intermittent Fever or Ague in passing through the Rideau Canal'. (71)

It must have been with mixed feelings that the passengers said farewell to their ship. It had been their home for 48 days and during that time no doubt, friendships had been formed, as adversity and hardship often encourage closeness. Also,of course, there may have been disagreements which had not healed. They might have had some affection for the ship in which they had suffered discomfort and hard times, and possibly some happy moments they would always remember. It was goodbye to their last link with England, and Captain Crawford and his crew, with whom they had lived and had got to know over the past weeks.

The Earl of Chichester, wrote from Stanmer 5 July 1834, to the *Sussex Advertiser*.

The Rev. Mr Sockett of Petworth has received a letter from the Superintendent of the party of Emigrants who sailed in the "British Tar". The letter which is dated Montreal, June 4th, states that the whole party had arrived at that port in good health and spirits, and also speaks highly of the conduct of the Emigrants. A few cases of measles had occured, which occasioned some delay at Grosse Isle owing to the Quarintine [sic] *Regulations. One woman named Ditton had been confined on board, and with her child was doing well.*

Upon the whole we have great reason to be thankful. The "British Tar" having left Portsmouth with one hundred and thirty-five Emigrants (some unwell) and arrived at Montreal with ***one hundred*** *and* ***thirty six****, all in good health and spirits.*

MONTREAL TOWBOAT COMPANY.

RATES OF TOWING VESSELS,

Exclusive of Pilotage,

BETWEEN

QUEBEC AND MONTREAL,

2: THE LAST LAP

We sailed from Spithead 17th April, with 135 passengers, and left the Land's End the 19th. The first land we saw was Cape Ray, in Newfoundland, on the 14th May, after a passage of only 25 days from leaving the Land's End. We arrived at Gross Island the 21st which is 30 miles below Quebec and came to Quebec June 1st. We were then towed to Montreal by a steam boat, 160 miles, in two days. We left Charles Townsend and several more passengers here that got work. I saw Charles Page, the saddler from Lewes, at Montreal; he was very well, and got plenty of work; we stayed here three days; this is a fine large town, and shops as large as any in Lewes. We here left the "British Tar" and were put in a packet-boat, and sailed to Kingston, about 200 miles in seven days, and then went on board a steam-boat and sailed up Lake Ontario to York, 160 miles. We stayed here five days, then started again for Blandford, about 90 miles further, where we are now. I saw W. Kemp and Gates the shoemaker at Ancaster, 45 miles from where I live, Kemp has got a very fine shop of business, keeping on two or three men. We arrived at Blandford 20th June, this is a very fine country as ever man set his foot on, and the people are very friendly, kind and obliging; here a man can find plenty of employment, and well paid for it, and a man that has got a family may do well here; each family of us are allowed five acres of land, with very high trees, that my gun will not kill birds off the tops of them. This is a very fine level country, and the best of land; here are as fine wheat and corn as ever I saw in England, pease in particular, the grass is very good, and mowers are in great request; land is selling here at 3,4, and 5 dollars per acre, allowing 4 or 5 years to pay it in. Henry and I intend to buy 100 acres very shortly. I have the pleasure to inform you we are all in good employment, I have plenty of work at shoe-making, and can earn three shillings and my board per day; Henry is working in a brick-yard at three pounds per month, board and lodging, washing and mending; Alfred is at service with Mr Birch, for six dollars per month, board and lodging, washing and mending, which is twenty- five shillings English; Richard I put apprentice to a blacksmith for five years, his wages will average twelve pounds per year, with board and lodging etc.

My Dear Friend, words cannot express the satisfaction I feel when I look around me and see my family so comfortably situated, and all in good health, and I sincerely thank Mr Hurly and Mr Rogers for their kindness in sending us here; we have neither of us had a day's illness since we have been here.

Henry Harwood writing to a friend in Lewes [72]

From Montreal onwards the *British Tar* party began to disperse. As Henry Harwood says, Charles Townsend, Charles Crossing, William Rackett and George Walden got work and left. Brydone said crossly that they went without permission. The young men may well have been tired of Brydone's strict discipline, or they may have heard of the fortunes to be made in the U.S.A., and the low price of land there. The P.E.C. and other emigration agencies were constantly afraid that assisted emigrants to Canada would skip over the border into the Republic. The Emigrant Department of Quebec stated that roughly one in ten of the emigrants into Quebec in 1834 did so within their first year [73] and more went after a year or two, as Abraham Muzzall was to do. Brydone did not think highly of the U.S.A. and took pains to paint a gloomy picture of the country

Every American thinks highly of his learning; speaks well of himself, and of his country; which he represents, as the best in the world. It were well if he stopped here; but alas! most Americans pride themselves on their sagacity, acuteness, and ingenuity, in over reaching their neighbours. Gold is the idol of almost every one of them: and few of those with whom the poor emigrant is likely to have transactions, are of a class to be scrupulous how they obtain it.

Every settler in the States must take an oath, by which he renounces his allegiance to his king, and native country (not so in regard to an American, settling in Canada). If he have been dissatisfied with the existence of things at home, he may perhaps not be averse to this, but let me inform him, that he will not find the boasted prairies of America like the meadows of England, the richest of the soil. The advantages of the most fertile regions of the States, are more than counter-balanced by the greater insalubrity of the climate when compared to that of Canada.

The English emigrant may rest assured, that he will not long feel himself satisfied, and comfortable, amidst American manners and customs, but will become disgusted with the "peculiar" system of liberty, and equality that prevails in the States, and will regret, when too late, the step he has taken.

The most respectable, and best informed of the Americans, are already tired of the child (Liberty) which they have reared; and although, from expediency, they still continue to nurse their bantling, are well convinced that a system of liberty and equality, so contrary to all experience, to every law human and divine, cannot long exist.(74)

As we have seen Brydone was to take his charges to Kingston by a route well away from the American border, via the River Ottawa and the newly opened Rideau Canal. This canal was built by the British Government to give a route north of the St. Lawrence river from the Chaudiere Falls on the River Ottawa to Kingston on Lake Ontario. It was intended to provide a military communication well away from the American border. It had taken six years to build under the charge of Lieutenant Colonel By of the Royal Engineers, and eventually cost over £1,000,000. There were 47 locks along its route linking existing rivers and lakes. Brydone was prudent to take a supply of quinine, for some of the navvies who had built the canal had died of malaria.

The *British Tar* emigrants' journey was not without incident. They were delayed for five hours at the start of their steamboat journey up the Ottawa river and William West procured some beer, got drunk and beat up Sarah Snelling. 'Cross and stubborn', he then set off on foot to return to Montreal and England leaving Mary, their seven children and the imminent new baby. Brydone and six men from the party went in pursuit and found William hiding in a bush. As an old smuggler, said Brydone, William was probably well used to hiding thus. The search party was re-united with the main group just as the tardy steamboat arrived. Perhaps it a was a combination of beer, frustration and strained relations built up during the journey that pushed William over the edge. Although the rigours of the sea voyage were over, this part of the journey was exhausting with constant early morning departures, much loading on and off various kinds of transport and one night stops with often rough and ready accommodation.

'Sometimes we were drawn by horses, sometimes tied to a steam boat along the new cut', wrote Cornelius.(75) Sometimes, when there were no horses available, the passengers pulled the boat themselves along a stretch of canal. Inspite of the upsets there does seem to have been a feeling of comradeship and enthusiasm amongst the *British Tar* party for they had no particular or urgent timetable to work to, and could just as well have waited for the towing horses. On 11 June when the party was spending a night on the grounded boat just before Chaffey's Mills, Mary West had threatening signs of labour and called Brydone out in the night. Fortunately, at this very inconvenient time her symptoms passed away.

After eight days towing from Montreal, they arrived at Kingston at 8 a.m. on 13 June. Everyone was said to be in perfect health. Brydone was relieved that he had not needed the quinine, nor any of the medicines he had taken from the medicine chest at Montreal. He treated every man and woman-including presumably William West- to a pint of beer, and every child to half a pint of milk, at a cost of 22s.6d. The steamboat *Coburg* was then engaged to carry the party across Lake Ontario to Toronto at a cost of 6s.6d. per person including baggage. Twenty women and the younger children had beds in the cabin. They arrived at Toronto at 3 p.m. on Sunday 14 June. Brydone then went to considerable trouble to procure cheese and bread for 58 people,and beer for 41.

Cornelius and his family were tempted to leave the party here, for as they drew in to Toronto Cornelius says 'We saw a gentleman on the wharf we thought we knew'. The pleasure of seeing familiar faces in this new land must have been acute. Henry Harwood must have had the same pleasure at meeting up with Charles Page, W.Kemp and

Gates 'the shoemaker'. Mr Gurnett, the man on Toronto quayside, came from Horsham; Elizabeth had been a Smallwood from Horsham before her marriage. Gurnett offered Cornelius and William work, but they were either pressurised or tempted by the Governor's offer of 5 acres of free land and a hut, and decided to continue to Blandford. Some of the young men, however, who were 'fit and willing' departed to work at canal building on the Grand River, or to the harbour at Kettle Creek, at wages of £2 to £3 per week. Brydone now apprenticed out some of those boys in his especial charge. The emigrants rejected the open shed on the beach allotted to them during their stay in Toronto and found lodgings for themselves. The Wests were offered a small house for Mary was still daily expecting her confinement. The luggage was stowed on the wharf.

Here in Toronto, the emigrants received drafts payable on the Canada Company for their money deposited with Brydone at the start of their journey. Cornelius later said that the family had only three guineas left by the time they reached Blandford. Brydone also paid Frederick Upton, who had acted as steward on the journey, the cook and others who had been 'useful in various capacities'. From this point onward the expenses of the party were paid by the Governor, who was anxious to settle the labourers at Blandford. Seventy men, women and children in family groups, 20 young men, the 'Rivers' family of eight who were travelling with them, the Ditton baby and Brydone, making one hundred in all, embarked on the Queenston steamboat for Hamilton at the head of Lake Ontario. Here they spent the night, some of the women in houses, and the rest lodging in a barn, sleeping on clean straw and hay. Edward and Henry Hammond went no further, for they got work at Oakville at 50s. and 40s. per month including board and lodging. The Uptons and George Morgan also got work and left, but Frederick Upton volunteered to help Brydone conduct the remainder of the party on the last lap of the journey.

Home was in sight. Cornelius says Brydone hired 20 wagons, Brydone himself says 14, to travel overland the final 50 miles from Hamilton to Blandford. Four wagons took the families as follows:

1 The Barton, Gamblin, Kemp and Martin families; 13 people

2 The Perring and West families; 12 people

3 The Coleman, Ditton and Green families; 12 people

4 The Rivers, Snelling and Voice families; 13 people

The men and older children presumably walked or rode with the luggage wagons. Wagon number 3 and some of the luggage wagons fell behind. At the last overnight stop, at Vanorman's Inn, Mary West went into labour only one day's journey away from her new home. When the party moved on the next morning they left her behind, with the young Elizabeth Voice to help a midwife deliver the child. Brydone does not record the name nor the sex of the new baby.

All Brydone's deep suspicions of Americans were reinforced by the conduct of the innkeeper's American wife. He had negotiated bread and milk for the children, tea and beds for the women and children, and a barn for the men and boys. Later in the evening the landlady brought out counterpanes to cover the boys in the straw. For these she intended to claim the price of extra beds. Brydone refused to pay. On settling the bill, however, Brydone found the landlady had doubled the agreed price for the milk she had supplied. To avoid any repercussions rebounding on Mary West and Elizabeth Voice, Brydone paid up admitting that the woman had defeated him.

On 11 a.m. on 21 June, the first of the wagons arrived at Blandford, 64 days after the travellers had left Portsmouth. The remainder of the wagons straggled in during the following 24 hours. The weary passengers were housed in barns until they were apportioned their land, and given help to build the basic structure of their huts. Brydone and Frederick Upton departed on a three week tour of the country, visiting previous P.E.C. emigrants en-route. On his return on 17 July Brydone was pleased to find that all the emigrants had got work; even the unfortunate Mr. Barton, who had aspired to become a church organist, only to find the new church had no organ. He had now been appointed schoolmaster and parish clerk.

Thomas Ditton, John Gamblin, William Martin, Coleman and Cornelius Voice had vied with each other in the building of their huts. Several of which had a ridged roof instead of the usual lean- to, or shanty roof. Thomas Ditton had thatched his with straw - apparently a novelty in Upper Canada. When Brydone left on 19 July, all the families were settled in their own huts. In spite of all his strictures about Americans Brydone was pleased to take a fast American Packet home, from New York to Liverpool in three weeks. He noted in his journal before he left that Cornelius 'told me it was impossible for him to express, how fortunate a circumstance his coming here had been: that himself, his two sons, and his nephew, were together, making six pounds per week.' Cornelius did not alter his opinion in the next 14 months, for in September 1835 he wrote home the letter reproduced on the following two pages.

Blandford, Upper Canada, Sept. 20th, 1835

Dear Brother and Sister,

This comes with our love to you, hoping it will find you all well, as thank God, it leaves us all. Cornelius has still a wound in his leg, but he is a great deal better. Brother, I should (have) wrote to you before; I wanted to get settled, to see how I like the country. We all like America very much, it is a pleasant country, particularly Blandford: there is a many settled round here, most English. We had a good passage over; we landed at Quebec the first of June, but our vessel came as far as Montreal: there we left and went on shore and staid two days, before our doctor could get a boat, as he was to see the whole party up to Toronto, Upper Canada, and that was where we paid our passage to. From Montreal to Toronto is 600 miles. We travelled in a large boat like a barge, up a new cut, and it being so much up hill, that we past through a great many locks. Sometimes we were drawn by horses, sometimes tied to a steam boat. We travelled this way 400 miles, to Kingston, there we left the boat and all got in a steam boat. We had 200 miles up to Toronto, 12th June. As soon as they stopt the steamer, we saw a gentleman on the wharf, we thought we knew, as soon as we got out, he came to us: he ask us if we did not come from Horsham. I said no, my name is Voice, from Billingshurst. He said his name was Gurnett from Horsham. He is living at Toronto, carrying on the printing business. He told me to come to him, he would help me to work: he got work for me and William. Before we begun our Doctor come to our lodging; he said he had been to the Governor, to speak for the party, and the Governor said the married men were to come to him, he (would) give 13 families each 5 acres of land, and build us a shanty as they call it, at Blandford, and take us there free of expence. Our doctor was sent with us: it is a 100 miles further up the country. We come 50 miles in the steamer to Hamilton, that was as far as we could come by water. Our doctor hired 20 wagons to carry us and our luggage the 50 to Blandford. We reached there the 21st June: we were all put in the 'squire's barn, while our houses were building. Our houses were built with round trees laid one on the other, with a few boards for the roof, without any door, or window, or fire place, we had to do the rest as we could. Our land was full of large high trees. We were in the barn just one month, and some were there longer. William and John went out the next day to get work, and got work for all. We get 6s 3d a day, English money. We were glad to begin work, for we had but 3 sovereigns. We soon earned some money, and then we all went to work at our house and land. We had a new brick chimney and oven, we have 2 pair of sashes, a front door, and a back door, and a good roof, and shingled: we have no tiles nor slates; we have got this done before the cold weather comes. We have cleared our 5 acres of land. The way we clear is, chop the trees down with an axe, then chop them in lengths, and draw them together with oxen, and burn them; this is a hard job to clear land, but thank God, we have done. Brother, now I will tell you what I have got, and what I have grown. I have got 4 cows, and 4 calves, them I am raising up: I have 4 sows, and 20 young hogs. There is plenty of beech-nuts, we are in hopes that they will be good pork, without any more fatting: we have about 100 fowls, little and big, besides geese and turkeys: we sell none but eat them all, for they are very cheap here. Your sister is making 20 pounds of butter a week. We have a good garden; plenty of potatoes, and we have all sorts of vegetables, cucumbers and melons grow on the ground, the same as cabbages; the other part of our ground with Indian Corn and Oats, for cows and other things in the winter. Our cows and hogs cost nothing in the summer, they run in the woods and keep themselves. I only wish you had been here last month, to see your sister and the girls making sugar in the woods, sometimes up to their knees in snow : but they made 150 lbs. of sugar , and 60 lbs. of treacle. The Yankees called it a good bunch, being a bad sugar year. Your sister has learnt to make her own soap and candles. Our house is about half a mile from the village. We have a new church, and (an) English preacher came up the day before we did. There was but two shops when we came here, but there is five more shops now built since we have been here, and about 50 framed houses. We can get any thing for money, the same as in England. Brother and sister, if you can get here, I think it would be a good thing for your family, as there is plenty of work for your boys, and girls, and good pay. The same doctor came out with Lord Egremont's vessel last April, as came out with us: he came to see us and told us he brought out 250 from Sussex: he settled all the families at Brantford, on a five acre lot each, the same as us. We came through Brantford about 25 miles back: he told us that he was coming out with another vessel load next April: he said that he was going to take them that liked to go, to farm a new tract at the side of Goderich, about 60 miles further up the country than we are. William and John has been up there: they said it was a lake, but rather unsettled. If you think of coming, I can get you a five acre lot near ours, as I am acquainted with the 'squire. You can change your money here, but you must get that settled at home: you had better go to Mr Sockett, at Petworth, and you may shew him this letter, and he will tell you the best way to get out. Go soon, as the vessel will start the beginning of April. We wrote home, but we have not received any letter from them, but we have had a letter from Mary. I staid at home to write to you. All four boys are gone to play a game of cricket:they play 11 on a side, 10s. to 5s. the trade against the gentlemen. I cannot tell you which beat, they are not come home. So I must conclude with all our loves to you, and all your family.

CORNELIUS AND ELIZABETH VOICE

I forgot to say that Elizabeth was married 18th July, to a young man, the name of Coleman: he came from England with us, they live on a 5 acre lot, joining ours. Brother, I hope you will write as soon you receive this. This letter is by the favor of a young lady that is coming home, she has been out on a visit to her sister.

Direct to me, Cornelius Voice, Blandford Town Plot, London District, Upper Canada, North America.[75]

3: PUSHED OR PULLED?

Why did Elizabeth and Cornelius, Mary and William West, Edward and Henry Hammond and their fellow passengers choose - if choose they did - to leave the land of their birth and seek a new life across the seas? Their reasons were many and varied.

The Hammonds, William West, Job Hodge and many of the emigrants were agricultural labourers and life for them in England in the 1820s and 1830s was hard. Sockett's description of the labourers' lot summed up their situation very well:

Here, however industrious and frugal, a labouring man may be, there is no longer a demand for his labor sufficient to enable him to bring up a family, without assistance from a parish; much less, to lay by any provision for old age: and, especially, if he marry, and have several children, he has no prospect before him but hard labor, and hard fare, during his youth and middle age, and the work-house in the close of his days.(76)

As Mary West said in her appeal to the East Hoathly Poor law Authorities her husband could not earn enough to support his family. Thomas Moody speaking, before the 1827 Select Committee on Emigration, of Shipley in West Sussex gave the average pay of the farm labourer there as 10s.a week.(77) Ten years later Sockett giving evidence before another Select Committee, this time on the 1834 Poor Law Amendment Act, confirmed this figure and in reply to a question referring to 'high' wages of 11s.6d. retorted indignantly 'I do not consider 11s.6d. a week high wages at the present price of corn'.(78)

Life for the labourer's wife was equally hard. She had few opportunities to supplement the family income in rural areas. Already often endowed with a large family she could do yet more washing for 8d.a day, earn a few coppers by stone picking or hop pole shaving, and help with the harvest. Moody, in his evidence to the 1827 Committee, estimated that during hay and cereal harvest a man's pay could increase from 10s. to 20s. a week, and his wife could possibly earn £5.4s. overall but he gave little expectation of any further earnings on the woman's part. Almost certainly, anything that a wife earned would have been taken into account in determining the amount of any parish relief the family received.

After the Napoleonic war, from 1815 onwards, there was a slump in farming prices coupled with wage reductions, a situation exacerbated by a steady rise in population and consequent unemployment. Farmers had no need to pay a living wage, for their workers could claim parish relief to bring their income up to a basic subsistence level. Such relief was largely determined by the provisions of the Speenhamland decision of 1795 when magistrates in Berkshire initiated a scheme of virtual family income supplement tied to the price of bread and paid out of the poor rates. By the 1830s, for example, the House of Industry on the Isle of Wight was paying typical out relief of 1s.6d.per child, per week, for every fourth child and more. With the benefit of hindsight it is difficult to appreciate why the initiators of the Speenhamland system did not foresee the implications of their albeit humanitarian decision. Employers were relieved of the need to pay a living wage; the burden of making up the shortfall fell on the rate payer in general, and the labourer became a pauper even if he was in full employment. The pressures of the growth of population and the demands on the poor rate can be clearly seen for example in Billingshurst where the population in 1801 was 1,164, by 1831 it had grown by nearly 50 per cent to 1,540. The expenditure in poor relief in 1803 was £1,851, by 1833 the parish was spending £2,654.(79)

The solution introduced by the Poor Law Amendment Act of 1834 was harsh in the extreme. Parish allowances for dependent children were abolished and the family was reduced to living on the weekly wage, or, in dire straits, going into the newly established Union Workhouse where husband, wife and children were separated, not only within the building but often within the neighbourhood. At Hellingly, for example, the men would stay in Hellingly but their wives and children were sent to Arlington. Sockett, in his evidence to the 1837 Committee, was especially outspoken in his criticism of the effect of the 1834 Act on the working married man and his family. The full provisions of this Act were not felt for some time after the *British Tar* departed but they were already being debated in Parliament in the spring of 1834 and people would have become increasingly aware of what was proposed. The coming restrictions of the new act may well have been clearly spelled out to William West and his family before he told East Hoathly Vestry he was 'willing' to emigrate.

Those not in employment were totally dependent on parish relief. Many of the men on the *British Tar* had been on intermittent parish work in common with the men from Hellingly. In 1831 the House of Industry on the Isle of Wight anxiously circulated its parish Vestries asking for suggestions for measures to reduce pauperism; to little avail. Parishes asked farmers to find work for paupers, and there were one or two schemes of spade husbandry; both of these measures to be paid for by the parish, and there was always road making. Walter Burrell, a member of Parliament for Sussex, giving evidence on the 15 March to the 1827 Committee on Emigration said that he himself was employing from 20-25 men digging stones to make a road of no consequence in order that they might be employed. The wage given to a single man employed as pauper labour, or unemployed, was 4s. or 4s.6d. a week. After the introduction of the 1834 Poor Law Act the single man would not be entitled to any such outdoor relief and, if able bodied, would be taken very reluctantly into the workhouse, where conditions were to be deliberately made less attractive than a man could theoretically earn for himself outside. Many parish authorities hoped he would go away.

Emigration was one answer. Another was migration to the growing towns and cities, and the industrial areas of the North. By 1837 the Poor Law Commissioners in Sussex were urging claimants to go to the cotton factories of Lancashire where at least their wives and children could get factory work even if they, the men, were largely unwanted and untrainable in new skills. Some emigrants must have deliberately chosen farming opportunities in Canada rather than alien urban industrial life at home. Another answer was to be work on the rapidly developing railways. In 1834 there was none in Sussex but by the end of the decade many men were to find employment as railway navvies.

If some of the passengers on the *British Tar* were pushed, as Cobbett claimed many emigrants were, by the miseries of poverty and unemployment others must have been pulled by the opportunities that Canada offered. Cornelius and Elizabeth had five growing sons and two daughters in need of work. Letters coming home from emigrants on earlier P.E.C. ships constantly spoke of the good opportunities for carpenters and skilled craftsmen. Perhaps it was the Voice sons and daughters, and Henry Harwood's growing boys who persuaded their parents to go. There was also the promise of land. Elizabeth Voice and the young Coleman, after their marriage, occupied a 5 acre plot near to that of the elder Voices; William Green was granted his 200 acres; Henry Harwood and young Henry were planning to buy 100 acres, purchases that would have been impossible for them in England. Martha Voice and the young Mary West, in their early teens, would probably have got work straightaway as servants, for Brydone said he had many enquiries for 'female servants' and 'little girls' directly the party arrived at Blandford.[80] Whether their situation would have been greatly better than in England is debatable. The shortage of female labour in general in Canada did favour wages and conditions. Certainly, Susanna Moodie grumbled at length at the uppishness and unreliability of servant girls in Canada compared to those at home - a complaint echoed by emigrants to other colonies. This uppishness of servants was a facet perhaps of that elevation to a social class of society far above that they before occupied, promised by Sockett. How true this elevation was is questionable. Cornelius, in his letter, still speaks of cricket matches between the gentlemen and trade. It may be that his children would cast off old social hierarchies more quickly than he.

One important opportunity offered by emigration was that of starting afresh from old stigmas of birth and background; of being labelled base-born or illegitimate, as William West was, and Henry and Edward Hammond possibly were. Emigrants could also leave behind the label of pauper and workhouse child. Another freedom may have been that of religious freedom from the established and often autocratic Church of England. Elizabeth and Cornelius had most of their children baptised at the Hayes Independent Chapel at Slinfold; a Congregational Church. The two youngest boys, George and Joseph, were christened at Billinghurst Parish church only when there was no longer a registered Congregational Minister in the area. Cornelius was a member of Billinghurst Vestry but the only apparent occasion on which he exercised his vote was in April 1833 over the issue of discharging the Vestry clerk, a Mr Puttock, from office. Cornelius with a show of independence voted unsuccessfully to retain the clerk, and in the subsequent election voted for the unsuccessful candidate, who received only his vote and one other.[81] Abraham Muzzall came from a Huguenot background and was himself a Particular Baptist. Job Hodge, of the Isle of Wight, had one son christened at an Independent Chapel, and the youngest, Francis, at a Meeting House in Barton Village.

Another pull for emigrants was the attraction of letters coming back from Canada. Cornelius Voice's letter and that of Henry Harwood encourage family and friends to follow them out, partly for their own sakes and partly because of the home sickness of the emigrants themselves; they do so wish to see their kith and kin again. The authorities were well aware of the strong pull that such letters could exert. Burrell, in his evidence to the 1827 Committee, said that although farmers and landowners would be only too glad to encourage emigration the labourers themselves expressed no great interest. He suggested that favourable reports coming home from those who did go might be a great inducement.[82] The P.E.C. was to publish letters from happy emigrants in local papers during the months before a ship sailed, Henry Harwood's was one, and also published collections of letters for sale, including that from Cornelius and Elizabeth. All these letters should be treated with a degree of caution. The Harwoods and the Voices were craftsmen and literate, and hence likely to do well. Emigrants who did not prosper might not have felt inclined to write home even if they could do so, and if they did the P.E.C. might not choose to publish their letters.

The P.E.C. published letters of its own. Sockett in his *Letter to a Member of Parliament* written in June 1833 and published in London and Petworth appealed to landowners and parishes to finance emigration. 'The first edition... being exhausted, we have thought it right to reprint it and as the Session of Parliament is approaching, I am anxious to give it extensive circulation', he wrote to the Duke of Richmond sending him six copies in the hope that 'you will dispose of them where they were most likely to be useful.'[83] Sockett outlined the Petworth plan stressing the economic and social benefits for emigrant and sponsor. Sockett later told the 1837 Committee how on 24 December 1831 he received a return from the Petworth Poor Law Authorities stating that 103 men were currently drawing relief. Showing the figures to Lord Egremont he said ' My Lord, these labourers have eaten me up and they will soon eat your Lordship if something is not done to stop it'[84] - the cry of a man who has received his rates demand! We hope that Sockett did not spoil Egremont's Christmas celebrations, but four months later the first ships under the P.E.C. scheme sailed from Portsmouth with 49 people from Petworth amongst the passengers on board. Sockett was to claim in 1837 that it was the 107 people who had emigrated from Petworth between 1832 and 1837 that had reduced poor law expenditure in the town from £1,401 in 1832 to £426 in 1836.[85]

Anxiety on the part of the authorities was not only economic. There were constant fears that Britain would follow Europe and be torn apart by revolution. The French revolution at the end of the 18th century was still very much in people's memories, re-inforced by the re-surgence of revolution in France and elsewhere in 1830. The Swing riots, rick burning, machine destruction, and sheep stealing in the 1830s came as a nasty reminder of the powers of an enraged and exploited people. Egremont, Richmond, Chichester, and many of the Lewes Emigration committee were local magistrates. Sockett recommending his *Letter* to Richmond went on to say,'This Parish has 16 individuals (all mere boys), beer shop boys, in gaol at this moment for various offences, and we have about 100 paid by the parish.'[86] An organised police force began to appear in Sussex towns during this period. Persuading the poor to emigrate, even paying them to do so, could have been a small price to pay for removing a potential nuisance and threat.

The authorities not only pushed but pulled. The colonial administrators were very anxious to build up a strong, loyal population in Upper Canada to offset the French presence in the country itself, and the troublesome Republic of the U.S.A. over the border. Many emigrants although willing to leave Great Britain had no desire to totally cut their links with their King and country - although many did, as Brydone feared. Canada was not too far and there was a possibility of transatlantic visits; Cornelius's letter was being taken back to England by one such visitor. Australia was so far away, and had the stigma of being a penal colony. Those already settled in Canada needed labour, skills and servants and looked to emigrant ships to bring them.

Cobbett was to rail against this promotion of emigration of the poor by the well to do, maintaining that the labourer was a prime producer of food and wealth, and was himself heavily penalised by taxes on food and household goods. Money that went to support a great many people who produced, in Cobbett's estimation, nothing:

> *... it is only the **working people** that these tax-eating vagabonds say are **too numerous.** They do not say, that the pensioners, the sinecure folks, the grantees, the allowance-folks, the half-pay-folks, the military academy folks, the **poor** parsons (whom we are taxed to relieve), the placemen, the taxing people, the fundholders, the swarms of clerks in offices; they do not say, that these endless crews of idlers, all of whom live upon the fruit of the people's labour; the tax eating vagabonds do not say, that **these** are **too numerous!***

calling for reform of government he goes on to say...

> *then you, who produce everything good, will have your just reward and due enjoyment in the country of your birth; and, let, the **emigration agents**, carry away the prostitutes, thieves, and others who will not work, to starve upon the rocks, or die amongst the swamps of Nova Scotia and Canada.*[87]

The colonies often accused the emigration agents of already doing the latter. The P.E.C. was at pains to point out how well regarded Lord Egremont's emigrants were.

Such emigration agencies were, in the early 1830s, like the P.E.C., locally inspired and funded. There had been sufficient national government interest to set up a Select Committee on Emigration in 1827 but its recommendation for a permanent Board of Emigration was not implemented. However,the Committee's work did lead ultimately to the appointment of an Emigration Commission in 1831, of which Richmond was a member. It had but a short life and was wound up the following year. The Commission offered advice and information and Emigration Officers were eventually stationed at some ports for this purpose; Portsmouth authorities said they did not see the need for one.

Under the Poor Law Amendment Act of 1834 the Poor Law Commissioners had the authority to sanction loans to parishes to fund emigration. This money to be repaid out of the rates over a period of five years at five percent interest. The first government moves to actively sponsor emigration during the 1830s were largely concerned with encouraging the 'honest, sober and industrious' to colonise the new territories of South Australia.[88] Powerful incentives were needed to persuade people to go so far, for Australia, with a very few exceptions, came very much third in the emigration league, in competition with the U.S.A. and Canada. Parliament raised the money to send suitable applicants to South Australia from land sales in the colony. These emigrants were sent on Government contracted and supervised ships. The regulations stipulated by the Government on such ships and the outcry over the horrors of the commercially run mass emigration to America in the 1840s very slowly led to the enforcement of new Passenger Acts, and better conditions on all emigrant ships. Improvements enhanced by the introduction of steam ships on the Atlantic passage and speedier journeys.

No Trifling Matter

In January 1840 the Colonial Land and Emigration Board was set up. Emigration, henceforth, was to become one of the great issues and interests of the 19th century. The P.E.C., Elizabeth and Cornelius Voice, Mary and William West, Mrs Ditton and her new baby, and all their fellow passengers on the *British Tar* were in the vanguard of this movement.

HERE AND THERE;
Or, Emigration a Remedy.

POSTSCRIPT

As this book neared completion Barbara Brydone, the great grandaughter of J.M. Brydone, the Superintendent on the *British Tar* kindly provided copies of previously unpublished letters. From this correspondence we now know that Sockett offered Brydone at least £80 as his fee for the trip with the possibility of it being £100 in all including expenses. For as yet unknown reasons Brydone was in 1834 in something of a dilemma as to whether to continue his career as naval surgeon. Sockett offered him this trip to Canada as time to consider his future, and also promised that he would use his influence with the Duke of Richmond which "might afford a chance of a staff appointment on your return". In the event Brydone was to take the next three P.E.C. ships to Canada in 1835, 1836, and 1837. When he was in Canada in 1835 Brydone reported in his journal that he met Mr Hemming, one of the 1834 emigrants, but gives no further news of him. Subsequently Brydone became Land Steward to Lord Leconfield , Egremont's heir, and lived in Petworth until his death in 1866.

KNOWN AND PROBABLE EMIGRANTS ON THE BRITISH TAR

Surname	First Name	Baptism	Age[1]	Parish of Baptism	Home District 1834	Occupation	Immediate Destination	Source
Alexander								N/V
Barton [2]	John	*June 1796*	*37*	Hellingly	Hellingly (E.S.)	labourer		E/AR 375/12/5
Barton	John					C/schoolmaster & parish clerk	Blandford	PHA 139
Barton Mrs							Blandford	PHA 139
Barton child 1							Blandford	PHA 139
Barton child 2							Blandford	PHA 139
Barton child 3							Blandford	PHA 139
Bassam	J						Kingston	N/V
Bassam Mrs							Kingston	N/V
Bassam child 1							Kingston	N/V
Bullen								N/V
Coleman	G						Blandford	N/V
Coleman Mrs							Blandford	N/V
Coleman son [3]							Blandford	N/V
Coleman child 2							Blandford	N/V
Coleman child 3							Blandford	N/V
Crossing	Charles				*I.O.W*		Montreal	N/V
Dighton	William							N/V
Ditton	Thomas				*Brighton*	labourer	Blandford	PHA 139
Ditton	*Tabittia*				*Brighton*		Blandford	PHA 139
Ditton child 1					*Brighton*		Blandford	PHA 139
Ditton child 2	*Mary*				*Brighton*		Blandford	PHA 139
Ditton child 3		b. 28.4.1834			British Tar		Blandford	PHA 139
Eade	George				Petworth(W.S.)	farmer		PHA 8618 f.25v
Gamblin	John						Blandford	PHA 139
Gamblin Mrs							Blandford	PHA 139
Grafenstein	young man				*London*			PHA 139
Green	William				Pulborough (W.S)	sergeant	Blandford	PHA 139
Green Mrs					Pulborough		Blandford	PHA 139
Green child 1	son				Pulborough		Blandford	PHA 139
Green child 2	son				Pulborough		Blandford	PHA 139
Green child 3	daughter				Pulborough		Blandford	PHA 139
Hammond	Edward	*2.4.1809*	*25*	*Hellingly*	Hellingly(E.S.)	labourer	Oakville	E/PAR 375/12/5
Hammond	Henry	*12.8.1815*	*18*	*Hellingly*	Hellingly(E.S.)	labourer	Oakville	E/PAR 375/12/5

Table

Surname	First Name	Baptism	Age[1]	Parish of Baptism	Home District 1834	Occupation	Immediate Destination	Source
Harwood	Henry				Lewes(E.S.)	shoemaker	Blandford	S/A. 8.9.1834
Harwood	Henry	18.4.1813	21	Lewes	Lewes	C/brickmaker	Blandford	S/A. 8.9.1834
Harwood	Alfred	2.4.1815	19	Lewes	Lewes	C/in service	Blandford	S/A. 8.9.1834
Harwood	Richard	7.6.1818	15	Lewes	Lewes	C/blacksmith	Blandford	S/A. 8.9.1834
Heasman	Henry				W.Grinstead (W.S.)			N/V
Hemming							Guelph	N/V
Hemming Mrs							Guelph	N/V
Hilton family					West Sussex			H/T. 1.5.1837
Hodge	Job	*June 1799*	*34*	*Godshill*	*I.O.W.*	labourer		N/V
Huntley	W						Guelph	N/V
Huntley Mrs							Guelph	N/V
Hutson	William				East Hoathly(E.S.)			E/PAR 378/12/3
Hutson	Elizabeth				East Hoathly			E/PAR 378/12/3
4 sons out of 6	William	2.6.1799	34	East Hoathly	East Hoathly			
	Jesse	23.12.1810	23	East Hoathly	East Hoathly			
	Frank	23.1.1814	20	East Hoathly	East Hoathly			
	George	21.1.1816	18	East Hoathly	East Hoathly			
	Trayton	b.16.7.1819	14	East Hoathly	East Hoathly			
	James	b.6.6.1823	10	East Hoathly	East Hoathly			
Kemp Mrs					*Lewes (E.S)*		Blandford	PHA 139
Kemp Miss					*Lewes*		Blandford	PHA 139
Kemp	young man				*Lewes*	*plumber*	Blandford	PHA 139
Kemp	young man				*Lewes*	*plumber*	Blandford	PHA 139
Martin	William						Blandford	PHA 139
Martin Mrs							Blandford	PHA 139
Morgan	George						Hamilton	N/V
Muzzall	Abraham	12.4.1834[4]	20	Brighton	Brighton (E.S.)	carpenter	Blandford	PHA 139
Parsons	James				Hellingly (E.S.)	labourer		E/PAR 375/12/5
Pelling	Peter				Hellingly	labourer		E/PAR 375/12/5
Pennicott	John				Washington (W.S.)			PHA 139
Perring	J						Blandford	PHA 139
Perrring Mrs							Blandford	PHA 139
Perring child 1							Blandford	PHA 139
Perring child 2							Blandford	PHA 139
Pulling	*Guy*				*Tillington (W.S.)*			W/PAR 197/31/5
Rackett[5]	*William*	*1809*	*25*	*I.O.W.*	*I.O.W.*		Montreal	N/V
Rapson Mr					*Lodsworth(W.S.)*			N/V

Surname	First Name	Baptism	Age[1]	Parish of Baptism	Home District 1834	Occupation	Immediate Destination	Source
Richardson	Samuel				Hellingly(E.S.)			E/PAR 375/12/5
Ripley	William	*3.9.1815*	*18*	*Hellingly*	*Hellingly(E.S.)*			E/PAR 375/12/5
Sheppard	George	boy			Egdean(W.S.)		Zorra	W/PAR 79/31/1
Snelling	Henry				*I.O.W.*	labourer	Blandford	PHA 139
Snelling	*Sarah*				*I.O.W.*		Blandford	PHA 139
Snelling infant	*Henry*	*1833*	*1*	*Newport*	*I.O.W*		Blandford	PHA 139
Squibb	William				I.O.W.		Blandford	N/V
Tarrant		young man						PHA 139
Townsend	George	*b.18.10.1814*	*20*	*Lewes*	*Lewes(E.S.)*		Montreal	N/V
Tutt	John	*10.6.1804*	*29*	*Hellingly*	Hellingly(E.S.)	labourer		E/PAR/375/12/5
Upton	Frederick	19.7.1809	24		Petworth(W.S.)		Hamilton	PHA 139
Upton	*Percival*	*25.7.1817*	*16*		Petworth		Hamilton	PHA 139
Upton	*Egbert*	*16.2.1825*	*9*		Petworth		Hamilton	PHA 139
Verrall Dr					Seaford		Downie	N/V
Voice [6]	Cornelius	23.9.1787	46	Billingshurst	Billingshurst(W.S.)	carpenter	Blandford	W/PAR 5/37/5
Voice	Elizabeth	19.7.1789	44	Horsham	Billingshurst		Blandford	W/PAR 5/37/5
Voice	William	6.1.1811	23	Slinfold	Billingshurst	carpenter	Blandford	W/PAR 5/37/5
Voice	Elizabeth	28.9.1817	16	Slinfold	Billingshurst		Blandford	W/PAR 5/37/5
Voice	Cornelius	12.9.1819	14	Slinfold	Billingshurst		Blandford	W/PAR 5/37/5
Voice	Martha	18.11.1821	12	Slinfold	Billingshurst		Blandford	W/PAR 5/37/5
Voice	George	9.1.1831		Billingshurst	Billingshurst		Blandford	W/PAR 5/37/5
Voice	Joseph	9.1.1831		Billingshurst	Billingshurst		Blandford	W/PAR 5/37/5
Voice	*John*				Billingshurst		Blandford	W/PAR 5/37/5
Voice nephew	*John*						Blandford	W/PAR 5/37/5
Walden	George				*I.O.W.*		Montreal	N/V
Warren	William				*I.O.W.*	labourer	Quebec	N/V
Warren	*Mary*				*I.O.W.*		Quebec	N/V
Warren infant	*William*	*18.8.1833*			*I.O.W.*		Quebec	N/V
West (alias Warden)	William	10.12.1792	41	East Hoathly	East Hoathly (E.S.)	labourer/smuggler	Blandford	E/PAR 378/12/3
West	Mary	1802	32	East Hoathly	East Hoathly		Blandford	E/PAR 378/12/3
West	Mary	1821	13	East Hoathly	East Hoathly		Blandford	E/PAR 378/12/3
West	John	1823	11	East Hoathly	East Hoathly		Blandford	E/PAR 378/12/3
West	Edward	1825	9	East Hoathly	East Hoathly		Blandford	E/PAR 378/12/3
West	William	1827	7	East Hoathly	East Hoathly		Blandford	E/PAR 378/12/3
West	Eleanor	1831	3	East Hoathly	East Hoathly		Blandford	E/PAR 378/12/3
West	Francis	1832	15m	East Hoathly	East Hoathly		Blandford	E/PAR 378/12/3
West child 8		June 1834			Canada		Blandford	N/V
Willett	*Blinder*[Belinda?]			*Tillington(W.S.)*				W/PAR 197/31/1

TABLE

Notes:

An entry in italic denotes circumstantial evidence

1. At time of sailing
2. These may have been one person but the Hellingly Records do not credit their John Barton with a wife and family
3. Married Elizabeth Voice in 1835
4. Registered at Salem Particular Baptist Church, Brighton. His mother and sister, both Prudence, joined him in 1836
5. A Robert Rackett, IOW, went to Canada in 1837
6. Another Voice family went from Billingshurst in 1836

Abbreviations:

b. born, other entries are dates of baptism

C/ occupation in Canada

E/ East Sussex Record Office

H/T. *Hampshire Telegraph*

N/V *Narrative of a Voyage*

PHA Petworth House Archives

S/A. *Sussex Advertiser*

W/ West Sussex Record Office

REFERENCES

1. T. Sockett, *A Letter to a Member of Parliament, containing a statement of the method pursused by the Petworth Committee in sending out emigrants to Upper Canada in the years 1832 and 1833...* (J. Phillips Petworth, and Longman and Co. London, 1833), 18
2. *List of Necessaries for Emigrants to Upper Canada*, West Sussex Record Office, (hereafter W.S.R.O.) MP 2554
3. Reports from the Select Comittee to Inquire into the Administration of the Relief of the Poor under the Provisions of the Poor Law Amendment Act... *Minutes of Evidence*, 9 March 1837, British Parliamentary Papers (IUP,1968)
4. J.C. Hale, Capt., *Instructions to Persons intending to emigrate, as to the domestic Articles they should take with them; the kind of Provisions they should lay in; and their Conduct on board Ship and during the Journey up the Country.* (J. Phillips, Petworth, 1833)
5. W.S.R.O. MP 2554
6. Select Committee on the Poor Law, *Minutes*, 9 March 1837
7. Ibid
8. W.S.R.O., Goodwood Ms 1473 f.196
9. T. Sockett, *Letter*, 17
10. T. Sockett, *Letter*, 16
11. W.S.R.O., Goodwood Ms 1473 f.196
12. D.N.B., Vol X1,1909, Lennox
13. *Memorandum of Agreement between the Revd.Thos. Sockett, Mr Thos. Crippes and Mr Wm. Knight of Petworth as a Committee on behalf of the Right Honorable the Earl of Egremont and Carter Bonus of London*, W.S.R.O., Petworth House Archives, (hereafter P.H.A.), 1068-1070
14. J.M. Brydone, *Narrative of a Voyage with a Party of Emigrants Sent out from Sussex in 1834 by the Petworth Emigration Committee...*, (Petworth and London, 1834), 3
15. W.S.R.O., Goodwood MF 71, 273
16. Society for the Promoting of Christian Knowledge (hereafter S.P.C.K.), *Minutes*, Vol 40, (1829-1834), 481
17. S.P.C.K., *Annual Report*, 1838
18. J.M. Brydone, *Narrative...*, 41
19. J.M. Brydone, *Narrative...*, 9
20. W.S.R.O., Goodwood Ms 1474 f.202
21. Pat Tripp, Laura Upton Newell, *The Upton Family of Sussex England and Ontario Canada*, (Ms, London, Ontario, 1981)
22. W.S.R.O., PAR 79/31/1
23. J.M. Brydone, *Narrative...*, 58. For information about Green see W.S.R.O. PAR 153/12/3
24. Brighton Provident District Society, *Minutes*, 11 Feb 1834, East Sussex Record Office, (hereafter E.S.R.O.), PAR 255 7/3/1
25. Henry Harwood, Letter in the *Sussex Advertiser*, 8 Sept.1834
26. E.S.R.O., *Non Parochial Registers of Sussex*, Vol 4. For information about the Muzzall family see Ernest L Muzzall, *The Family of Abraham Muzzall Huguenot Descendant and Emigrant to America in 1834*, (1965), W.S.R.O.
27. For information about the West family see E.S.R.O. PAR 378/12/3 and PAR 378/35/4
28. J.M.Brydone, *Narrative...*, 15
29. For information about these men see E.S.R.O. PAR 375/12/5 and PAR 375/31/2/7
30. *Portsmouth Portsea and Gosport Herald*, 26 June 1831
31. *Portsmouth Portsea and Gosport Herald*, 22 May 1831
32. Isle of Wight County Records Office, *House of Industry Weekly Minute Book*, 2/HO/26
33. *Hampshire Telegraph and Sussex Chronicle*, 21 April 1834
34. Ibid
35. *Portsmouth Portsea and Gosport Herald*, 26 June 1831
36. *Brighton Patriot and Lewes Free Press*, 12 December 1837
37. Isle of Wight County Records Office, Index of births, deaths and marriages
38. *Portsmouth Portsea and Gosport Herald*, 21 June 1834
39. W.S.R.O., Goodwood Ms 1474 f.54
40. W.S.R.O., Goodwood Ms 1474 f.206
42. W.S.R.O., Goodwood Ms 1474 f.27
43. *Brighton Patriot and Lewes Free Press*, 28 Nov 1837
44. *Letter to the Rev. T. Sockett from an unknown writer* [Brydone] *from the St Lawrence River 22 May 1834*, W.S.R.O., P.H.A. Emigration 139
45. Ibid
46. *The Log of the England*, 1833, W.S.R.O., P.H.A., Emigration 138
47. 'Comforts on the Voyage', *The Times*, 6 March 1835
48. J.M. Brydone, *Narrative...*, 41
49. Ibid
50. T.Sockett, *Letter...*, 18
51. Ibid
52. W. Cobbett, *Advice to Young Men...*, 'Advice to a Father'
53. R.L. Stevenson, *The Amateur Emigrant*, (1st published 1895, Hogarth Press, 1984), 15
54. W.S.R.O., P.H.A., Emigration 139
55. Ibid
56. Ibid
57. Ibid
58. W. Cobbett, *Cottage Economy*, (1821), Paragraph 158
59. J.M. Brydone, *Narrative...*, 8
60. Tony Wales, *A Sussex Garland*, (1979, Godfrey Cave Associates)
61. 'Comforts on the Voyage', *The Times*, 6 March 1835
62. Hannah Glasse, *The Art of Cookery Made Plain and Easy*, (1796)
63. W.S.R.O., P.H.A. Emigration , 139
64. Ibid
65. Ibid
66. H.I. Cowan, *British Emigration to North America*, (1961), 156
67. J.M. Brydone, *Narrative...*, 12
68. Susanna Moodie, *Roughing it in the Bush*, (First published in U.K. 1852), A Visit to Grosse Isle.
69. P.H.A. Emigration, 139
70. Letter from Henry Harwood, *Sussex Advertiser*, 8 Sept 1834
71. List of Medicines purchased for the British Tar, W.S.R.O., P.H.A. Emigration 140
72. Letter from Henry Harwood, *Sussex Advertiser*, 8 Sept 1834
73. Figures issued by the Emigrant Dept., Quebec, 12 Dec 1834.
74. J.M. Brydone, *Narrative...*, 54
75. W.S.R.O., PAR 5/37/5
76. T. Sockett, *Letter...*, 16
77. Select Committee on Emigration from the United Kingdom, 1827, *Minutes*, 27 Feb 1827, B.P.P. (I.U.P., 1968)
78. Select Committee on the Poor Law 1837, *Minutes*, 9 March 1837
79. T.W. Horsfield, *History of Sussex*, (1835, this ed. Dorking 1974), 80
80. J.M. Brydone, *Narrative...*, 28
81. W.S.R.O., PAR 21/12/5
82. Select Committee on Emigration from the United Kingdom, *Minutes*, 15 March 1827
83. W.S.R.O., Goodwood Ms 1473 f.74
84. Select Committee on Poor Law, *Minutes*, 9 March 1837
85. Ibid
86. W.S.R.O., Goodwood Ms 1473 f.74
87. W. Cobbett, *Twopenny-Trash*, No.10, 238
88. *The Colonisation of South Australia*, British Parliamentary Papers, 4, Australia 1830-36, 499